MIKE WILLIAMS • ALMA THO

PLAY THE EXAM AME

ORMANCE WITH CONFIDENCE
ILL LOOK AFTER ITSELF!

UREATE · PRESS

DEDICATION
To David and Lesley,
the England Schools Rugby Players,
and Sevenoaks School students
who have been involved with
the development of this programme

ACKNOWLEDGEMENTS

The authors would like to thank many people who in their different ways, have contributed to the preparation of Play The Exam Game. Students; Jan McLintock, Natasha Brook-Walters, Emma Hogg and Jonathon Ions. Teachers and colleagues; Tony Stuart, Nigel Connell, Jane Billing, Mark Pyper, Peter Winter, Ian Dorton , Vanessa Sawyer and Midge Adams. Friends; Malcolm Severs, Bob Ogley and Maggs. Frank Keating and the editor of The Guardian, Peter Preston, for allowing us to reproduce the text of the article on Graham Gooch. David Bashford for his support and, David Noble for his patience and creativity in designing the book and its cover. David Lea for his poignant advice, and Honor MacMillan, Viv Grant, Suzy Jackson, Gill Sawyer, Lorna Evans and Mo Dobson for their unstinting support.

Design/artwork: David Noble
Cover concept and photography: David Noble
Illustrations: David Farris
Typeset in Leawood Book: Laserset, Derby.
Printing: Lakeside Printing, Sevenoaks, Kent

Published by The Baccalaureate Press
Sevenoaks, Kent
First published 1994

ISBN: 0 9522904 0 5

ABOUT THE AUTHORS

MIKE WILLIAMS, previously Head of Economics and Business Studies at Eltham College and Denstone College, has taught for the past twenty years at Sevenoaks School. During this time he has been an 'A' Level Economics examiner, a member of working parties assessing exam questions, a Tutor Counsellor at the Open University, a tutor at Wolsey Hall and the National Extension College, and has written texts for the Manchester Economics Project and Heinemann series Studies in the British Economy. A Rugby Football Union Senior Coach since 1981 – his book *Rugby Sevens* (Faber) was the first book on this popular form of the game – he has coached England Schools teams at 16, 18 and 19 age groups, during which time the performance enhancement skills of Alma Thomas were used at 16 Group level.

ALMA THOMAS, a qualified teacher and psychologist, has had 30 years experience of teaching in Primary and Secondary Schools and in Higher Education. Her last post in Higher Education was as Head of School of Human Movement Studies at Bedford College. She now works as a Performance Enhancement Consultant and has practices in London and New York where she works with elite sports people, international sports teams, corporate managers, performing artists including, opera singers, actors and musicians. She is still very involved in Education and works nationally and internationally for schools, teachers, and their managers. She is married and has two children at university.

CONTENTS

INTRODUCTION

Exams are just another GAME 10
Look after your Performance – and the result will look after itself 11
A Programme of Total Preparation 15
Performance Case Study – Graham Gooch 18

THE PROGRAMME

Introduction to the Programme 22

STAGE 1: PLANNING

YOU: THE PERSON 26
The Success Cycle 28
Self Concept 29
Self Enhancement Skills: 31
1. Self talk 31
2. Positive self talk or Affirmations 33
Motivation 36
Motivation Strategies: 37
1. Personal Contracts 37
2. Having a Change 38
3. Goal Setting 38
4. Imagery 42
Mental Rehearsal 44
Are you feeling Anxious? 45
Relaxation 48
YOU: THE STUDENT 50
How do you learn and study? 50
Questionnaire 1: How good a Student are you? 52
Questionnaire 2: What are your best methods of learning? 53
A Learning Map 55
Your Physical Well-being during Exams 56
Your Study Environment 57
The Importance of Time Control 61
The Importance of Memory 61
Concentration and Dealing with Distractions 63
What expectations do you have? 68
Fear of failure? 71
Planning your route map 72

STAGE 2: ORGANISATION

Introductory Themes 78
Getting Started 79
Organising: 80
Your Study Place 80
Your Life 81
Your Time 83
Your Work 83
Writing Your Performance Scripts 84
Where to Start? 89
Should the Performance Script be learnt at this stage? 98

STAGE 3: FAMILIARISATION

Introductory themes 100
The Rules of the Game 104
What to do in the Familiarisation Stage 113
What If's . . . 119

STAGE 4: LEARNING

Introductory Themes 122
Memory Skills 124

STAGE 5: PERFORMANCE

Introductory Themes 128

Outside the Exam Room 130
External:
Your Work 130
Your Recreation 131
Your Friends 131
Your Close Relationships 131
Your Physical Activities 131
Your Performance Routines 133
Internal:
Your Mental Skills 134
Post Mortems 135
Pre Performance Routines 136
Inside the Exam Room
Strategies for Performance 139
Controlling Your Exam Performance 140
Controlling the Start 141
Selection 142
Planning 142
Work 143
Pace 144
Time 144
Feelings 146

APPENDIX

1. STUDY SKILLS
Notemaking 150
Writing Draft Answers 151
Types of Exam Questions 152
Essay Writing 157
1. Writing Essays during course work 157
2. Writing Essays in Exams 158
Essay Direction Words 161

2. MENTAL SKILLS
Time Management Schedule 162
Answers to Questionnaire One 162
Problem Solving Models 164
Coping – A Self Help Approach 166
Glossary of Mental Skills 166

3. PRACTICES
Mock Exams 167
Practice Exams 171

4. PARENTS
Tips for Parents 171

5. ADDRESSES OF EXAMINATION BOARDS 174

PREFACE

The confidence Alma and I have in *Play The Exam Game* derives from three directions – my own successful response to an exam crisis from which the programme originates, proven theoretical knowledge, and the experience of a large number of students (and elite performers in other fields) who have embraced its principles and philosophy.

That exams are 'just another game' dawned on me when, after fourteen years teaching, I studied for a Diploma in Management Studies at London's Central Polytechnic. The discovery that by employing the right tactics – 'working smarter rather than harder' – I could gain such power and control over my performance gave me such a buzz, that not only did I enjoy my exams for the very first time, but I passed with flying colours.

I USED YOUR TECHNIQUES FOR MY OTHER SUBJECTS TOO, WHERE THEY WERE MOST USEFUL. I WAS REALLY WORRIED BY SPANISH LITERATURE, BUT WHEN YOU SPOKE ABOUT HOW YOU WENT THROUGH YOUR EXAMS, I REALISED THAT I COULD AFFORD TO DROP ALL THE MARKS ON THIS PAPER, – 20% OF THE EXAM – AND STILL DO WELL, PROVIDED THAT I PERFORMED WELL ENOUGH ON THE OTHER PAPERS. YOUR APPROACH ALSO HELPED ME IN DESIGN.

Dan, Grade A, 'A' Level, 1991

'If my own students employed the same tactics' I thought, 'surely they too could achieve results beyond even realistic expectations.' Focusing firmly on the student being in control of his/her own performance, rather than the work, I began fashioning a programme that involved a range of skills beyond specialist knowledge and the usual exam techniques.

I had been Chief Coach to England Schools 16 Group rugby team for five years before Alma joined the coaching team. In her role of team psychologist she introduced me formally to the mental skills required to give consistent and planned performances. 'Can't these principles be applied to exam performances as well as rugby matches Alma?' I asked. 'Of course they can,' she replied. From that moment the programme of exam preparation began to be enhanced by a more structured input of knowledge.

Three years later this much enhanced programme was featured in an article in The Guardian entitled 'A Levels? Just a Piece of Cake' and on BBC Radio 5. After reading the article the Headmaster of a major independent school wrote 'I greatly enjoyed the article . . . are you marketing the course?

PLAY THE EXAM GAME is the result.

HOW TO USE THIS BOOK

Success in any game is attributable to the skills and attitude of the individual performer, the Exam Game is no different. There are as many successful ways to prepare for performance as there are students to perform.

Play The Exam Game has not been written as a textbook, every page and every word of which has to be read by everyone. It is a handbook, a manual and a workbook designed to support and guide students – all of whom have uniquely different needs, life and learning styles – through each stage of their preparation. As a result there are many different ways to use *Play The Exam Game*. You will be able to find your own best way. Here are a few suggestions to start you off:

1. READ FROM COVER TO COVER

Reading the book from cover to cover will allow you to appreciate the philosophy, the themes and the principles which underly the programme, as well as the range of techniques which can be within your armoury. If time allows, it is a good idea to do this well in advance of starting your own preparation, so that during it, selective re-reading can take place.

2. READ STAGE BY STAGE

The programme has been organised into five stages each of which build cumulatively on its predecessor. You will find it useful to read about each stage before beginning your own work within it.

3. USED AS A REFERENCE MANUAL

You may wish to use the book as a reference manual, to re-discover techniques and reassure yourself of sections of text. Do this by using the contents, the glossary and the system of cross referencing.

4. USED AS A WORKBOOK

It has been designed with wide margins, in which the text can be annotated for easier reference, and a series of questionnaires, organisation charts, self assessment exercises and study skills which allow you to become actively involved in your preparation. So, feel free to write over the pages. It's your preparation workbook, no one else's!

EXAM SUCCESS DOES NOT JUST DEPEND ON YOUR IQ, HOW CLEVER YOU ARE, OR HOW CLEVER YOUR TEACHERS SAY YOU ARE! EXAM SUCCESS REQUIRES A WIDER RANGE OF SKILLS, ALMOST ALL OF WHICH YOU POSSESS ALREADY.

SO THROW AWAY THE TRADITIONAL ATTITUDE TO EXAMS, LEARN TO PLAY THE EXAM GAME AND CULTIVATE THE WINNING EDGE

INTRODUCTION

EXAMS ARE JUST ANOTHER GAME

Shakespeare understood: he wrote 'All the world's a stage, and all the men and women merely players'. Games, which are a part of our lives from the day we are born to the day we die. They interest and excite us tremendously. Everyone plays them, and when the outcome is important, we play to win.

We play because when we succeed, the feelings we have about ourselves are really good, but that even if the result is less than we hoped for, we will still enjoy the fun of taking part, of accepting the challenge to see if we can succeed. Louise Chunn, Editor of Guardian Women has written 'that (uncertainty) is one of the reasons why sex holds such a sway over us: it's an adventure fraught with uncertainty, charged with potential. It is almost never a sure thing'.

Games challenge our abilities and extend our frontiers. They allow us to discover not only how good we are, but how good we can become. Once the challenge, arising either from the game itself, or from competing players, is accepted, by using knowledge and skill to make decisions, moves and counter moves at each turn of the game, players compete to determine the outcome which, being uncertain and unpredictable to the end, adds immeasurably to the fun and excitement. The Exam Game certainly requires knowledge and a wide range of personal skills. The exam papers, with their variety of questions and problems, determine the challenge, and because they are unknown before the exam, they add the degree of uncertainly which is vital to the excitement of any game.

But can exams ever be really fun? Yes they can. If you ask this question you are only asking the same question that all potential champions ask themselves when, facing an important championship, they realise the hours and hours of training and practice to which they must commit themselves. Just as exercise isn't only abut physical hardship but is an opportunity to become 'all I capable of being', exams too are simply another opportunity for people to use and show their abilities.

Let's face it – exams aren't going to go away. They have to be taken. By treating exams as a game, we are not only able to be more positive in our preparation but better able to cope with the exam situation.

THE EXAM GAME REQUIRES YOU TO GIVE A PERFORMANCE

Exams are a particular performance situation. They are formal and public and the result really matters. The student has to produce quality work, performed at high intensity, against the clock, at a specified time and place, in a specified way, before a largely unseen audience, many of whom hold expectations about the result only marginally less fiercely than the students themselves.

Exams are a challenge, but they are also a terrific opportunity to display all the skills and qualities you possess – personal, physical and mental – rather than just a narrow range of technical skills Your results are determined by your performance. Performances involve both internal and external elements. Both need to be understood at an early stage.

LOOK AFTER YOUR PERFORMANCE – AND – THE RESULT WILL LOOK AFTER ITSELF !

INTERNAL ELEMENTS OF PERFORMANCE

All performances begin with you, and what you want to achieve – your objectives. You, not the work should be centre stage. The skills and qualities which distinguish the successful performer from the less successful are usually NOT the talent, but the desire, the responsibility, the drive, the discipline and the persistence. Using these personal qualities, many less talented students achieve, while many potentially more gifted, perform less well.

YOU

YOUR KNOWLEDGE → **YOUR THINKING** → **YOUR PERFORMANCE** → **YOUR RESULTS!**

determines determines determines

YOUR THINKING: YOUR ATTITUDES

Your thinking is important because of its direct link not only with your behaviour, but the energy you inject into your behaviour.

THE IMPORTANCE OF DIFFERENT ATTITUDES

Statement →	**Message** →	**Behaviour outcome**
"I always find exams difficult."	The same thing will happen again.	Lack of Motivation
"Exams are something which has to be gone through, and I will succeed."	Acceptance of the challenge. I have to do it so I might as well do it well.	I will plan and organise thoroughly. I will do the best I can.

The attitudes we hold, and carry as our personal baggage through life, are an amalgam of beliefs, thoughts, feelings, ideas – what we call our 'self talk' – born from our own experiences, from hearing statements of other peples' lives, and, most potently, statements about ourselves, sometimes buried deep in our sub-conscious – by friends, parents, teachers and people who have known us.

OUR ATTITUDES ARE OUR CHOICE

Dr David Lewis, a clinical psychologist at Susses University, who holds regular de-stressing workshops for examination candidates states: 'A great fear of examinations seems to have been built into us from an early age. You have to bear in mind that there is nothing you cannot achieve, that you need only ordinary intelligence levels to pass most exams, and that if you build up your confidence through adequate preparation, there is simply nothing to fear.'

The choice we make is under our control. We can choose to be positive about ourselves, or we can choose to be negative.

YOUR SELF TALK

Your self talk is crucial in determining your attitude. It can be dangerous and negative, or it can be stimulating, kind, helpful and positive.
We can be negative about ourselves, our performance and our performance preparation, making the whole task so much more difficult, or we can be positive making the whole task so much easier and more enjoyable.

Deciding to be positive is one thing, maintaining it is another. All human beings, even the most successful, experience both negative and positive thoughts every day of their lives. Positive thoughts do not develop by themselves, they have to be deliberately nurtured.

One American psychologist has compared the human mind to a garden in which the gardener lavishes meticulous care on his flowers and shrubs, tending the soil, turning it over, fertilising it. Yet, in the very same soil, without any effort at all, weeds not only grow, but proliferate, without reference to the grand plan of the gardener. Once chosen, positive thoughts require continual reinforcement by our self talk – the words we speak to ourselves every day our our lives.

THE IMPORTANCE OF ALL YOUR SKILLS AND QUALITIES

Students invariably know far more than they manage to write in an exam. Often too they perform better in practice than they do in the exam. Tony Buzan reminds us of this in his book 'Use of Memory':

'I remember at least three students in my undergraduate years, who knew more about certain subjects than practically anyone else in the year and who consequently used to give private tutoring and coaching to those who were struggling. Extraordinarily, these bright students would regularly fail to excel at examination time . . .' The experience of Buzan's students – which may well remind you of some stressful and panicky experiences of your own – illustrates that an exam performance requires a much wider range of skills (and qualities) than just knowledge and its use.

The Technical skills which are specific to any one subject – the knowledge of your subjects, their ideas, concepts and theories and the use of this knowledge to answer exam questions – are vital of course. Without the specific knowledge there isn't a performance at all.

Organisational skills are the ability to plan, organise and manage a range of elements – work and time being but two – throughout preparation and performance, while **physical skills** are the ability to maintain physical well-being despite the fact that your body is being severely tested by hours of preparation and exertion in the exam room.

Mental skills (self confidence, motivation, relaxation, concentration, and the ability to control distractions and anxiety) and **personal qualities** (patience, determination, persistence) can be harnessed to develop coping strategies, which allow the student to control not only the technical elements of their performance, but every situation in which they find themselves. When these wider performance elements are incorporated within a student's performance preparation, their feelings of control and confidence increase immeasurably.

This departmental memo, commenting on the prospects of four 'A' Level students shows the importance of taking all of a students' skills into account. Assessed narrowly, using only technical skills, none appeared to have much of a chance. Yet the final grades each student achieved (entered in the right hand margin) fully vindicated my own – more widely assessed – predictions.

MEMO
To: Head of Economics / Sevenoaks School

Date: 2nd May 1989

Business Studies Predicted Grades

I find Mike's grades in some cases way out of line.

Sarah is not going to get a B. She only started working around the Easter holidays. (C)

I had to see Richard's parents after the mock exams, when they admitted that he had done scarely any work over the last 15 months. How a B is going to arrive I don't know. (B)

Paul may just about scrape through with a D on a good day - his coverage of the syllabus is very selective and he has got a remarkable capacity to go right off tangent. (A)

I shall eat my hat if Lisa passes the exam. Her numerate work is appalling; she can neither add nor subtract, let alone do anything more sophisticated, and her written work is very, very pedestrian. (A)

EXTERNAL ELEMENTS OF PERFORMANCE

THE ROLES OF THE EXAMINER

Examiners play two roles in The Exam Game – designers and arbiters.

In designing the paper, the Chief Examiner determines the precise nature of the performance and the precise range of skills required to perform well. In this he plays a similar role to the designer of any game. Without a course a golfer would be unable to play. There would be no game, no challenge and no fun. The same would apply if all golf courses were identical – very quickly they would cease to be either an interest or a challenge.

The Examiner is challenging you to find your way to perform well, the kind of challenge that is usually exciting rather than terrifying. He and his team of Assistant Examiners mark the paper and award grades.

THE GOALS OF THE EXAMINER

If the opportunity offered by the exam is to be taken full advantage of, knowledge of an Examiner's goals and the methods used to achieve them, is of prime importance. Such knowledge is often not available to students. However, we interviewed a Chief Examiner whose answers are given over page:

1. What are your objectives as an Examiner?
'To ensure that as many people as possible, who reach the required standard, pass the exam.'

2. How do you achieve this?
'Examiners design questions which give a student an opportunity':

a) To show knowledge of the syllabus.
b) To show their understanding of the syllabus.
c) To show their ability to write in a logical and organised fashion.
d) To show their ability to handle ideas and to be able to use knowledge to support an argument
e) To show their ability to write 'to time' under exam conditions.

3. How are the questions designed?
'The syllabus, the recommended textbooks used by students during the course, as well as collections of past papers, are used to design questions of an appropriate style and standard to previous years.'

'Some parts of the syllabus are so important that they have to be examined. Of the remainder, some sections have a higher priority than others.' These words are reiterated by the Associated Examination Board (AEB): "In setting the papers the Chief Examiners take the syllabus as gospel."

THE UNKNOWN AND UNCERTAINTY

All games have elements of uncertainty, exams are not an exception. When the balls break at the beginning of a snooker match, the second player, despite having a general idea, does not know precisely where they will come to rest. His role is to wait, and only then respond within a definable range of options, to the problems posed by the first player. Before the pages of the exam paper are turned in the exam room, the precise nature of the questions remains unknown. Both situations, games and exams, require a heightened emotional state which varies from individual to individual.

Good performers use these emotions and performance situations to their advantage. People who regularly perform in public, who constantly experience the pressure of preparation and the tension arising from expectations of their performance – actors, musicians, public speakers, sports stars and rock stars – use these feelings of pressure and stress to enhance their performance to well above their normal standards. Harnessing such powerful feelings to your own use, learning to manage them to bring your performance to a fine edge – just as other great performers, many of whom you admire, do on other fields and platforms – is one of the most enjoyable challenges of The Exam Game.

LUCK

GARY PLAYER, THE WORLD FAMOUS SOUTH AFRICAN GOLFER, CONGRATULATED BY A HAPPY FAN WHO SUGGESTED "YOU'RE A LUCKY .. .." REPLIED, "I AM LUCKY – AND DO YOU KNOW, THE MORE I PRACTICE THE LUCKIER I BECOME."

Luck, as it is understood by the postcard industry is, like lucky charms, an external element of performance. It is therefore outside your control. Students who put their faith in such external elements are really admitting their helplessness, thereby increasing their own feelings of stress.

MAKING YOUR OWN LUCK

The luck we make for ourselves, the internal luck we make by our own qualities and behaviour – our ability to think of the right things and be focused enough to do them – is quite different. The New Zealand All Blacks, internationally renowned for decades as a successful team, say:

'IT'S NOT PRACTICE THAT MAKES PERFECT:
IT IS PERFECT PRACTICE THAT MAKES PERFECT'

Developing your own luck is not magic, nor is it effortless. Your luck is under your control: it is your responsibility – no one else is involved!

A PROGRAMME OF TOTAL PREPARATION

WHY PREPARATION

Successful performances, determined by personal qualities and behaviour are always prepared for, planned and practised. They are rarely accidental. Preparation is the foundation of your success.

Your exams will be over in a matter of hours, but your preparation will last mch longer – maybe weeks or months. The programme should be carefully designed:

- To be under your control, not anyone else's
- To satisfy your needs, not anyone else's
- To make everything as "easy for you" as possible
- To be as "enjoyable" as possible **and particularly**
- To increase your confidence and self esteem.

IF YOU DO THE RIGHT THINGS, PRACTICE THE RIGHT THINGS IN THE RIGHT WAY – YOU INCREASE YOUR CHANCES OF SUCCESS

HOW TO PREPARE TOTALLY

YOU will be the focus of your performance in the examination room. Therefore YOU not THE WORK TO BE DONE should be centre stage.

Most revision programmes look backwards revisiting old work, rehashing old material, concentrating mainly on the technical skills and knowledge, rather than looking forward to the final performance where a much wider range of skills will be required. Often some of the deepest problems of performance have little to do with the technical elements.

BY FAILING TO PREPARE YOU ARE PREPARING TO FAIL

CONSIDER A TYPICAL PRE "A" LEVEL PARENTS MEETING

During the evening 18 parents talked through the problems and prospects of their sons and daughters. Only 25% were concerned with intelligence, cleverness, knowledge and academic ability. 75% were concerned with their sons or daughters personal skills – the mental skills we all already possess which play a crucial role in exam performance.

'My son drifts through lessons'	(Concentration Skills)
'He is lazy and is coasting'	(Motivation Skills)
'She can sit for three hours in an exam without a word being put on paper'	(Anxiety Control)
'She gets far too aroused – and panics'	(Arousal Control)
'He is superficial. He works far too quickly: he is overconfident'	(Confidence)
'He lacks confidence. He talks himself to a poor performance.'	(Self Talk)
'He has a very low opinion of himself.'	(Self Talk)
'Cars are a terrific distraction. He is car crazy'	(Goal Setting)
'Time just seems to drift by without work being done.'	(Time Management)
'He finds it very difficult to start'	(Switch On Skills)

SUCCESSFUL PEOPLE MAKE A HABIT OF DOING WHAT UNSUCCESSFUL PEOPLE DON'T WANT TO DO! ANDREW WHO TOOK HIS A LEVELS IN 1993. "PREVIOUSLY I SPENT HOURS ON AREAS OF THE SYLLABUS I ENJOYED OR COULD DO WELL ALREADY. BY CONTINUALLY REPEATING 'SUCCESSFUL PEOPLE MAKE A HABIT . . .' I KNUCKLED DOWN TO THE AREAS I DIDN'T ENJOY."

Such comments are very familiar – perhaps people have even said them about you? If they have, how do you feel? What have you done about it? What can you do? The answer is PREPARE TOTALLY: Good exam performances like any other performances require the integration of a totality of skills – technical, mental, physical and organisational.

WORK SMARTER NOT HARDER

Hard work paid off for Duncan; it will help you too. Yet, mindless work, just for the sake of working, or pleasing other people is neither enjoyable nor constructive. Time serving never is. Make sure the exam game is played your way.

The hardest and yet the most obvious lesson I learnt about A-Levels is that you have to work hard to pass them. Unfortunately, I didn't fully appreciate what 'hard work' meant until very late, although possibly enough to still pass with resonable grades.

I discovered that working hard did not merely mean completing homework on time. It involved going that little bit further in an attempt to gain a better grade, finding the motivation to adhere to a strict revision timetable, and finding the determination to dedicate myself fully to my work, for what was after all only a very small piece of my life. When finally all of this was over, the sense of acheivement I felt more than made up for it.

DUNCAN

P.S. Good luck with the book - I'll be buying it!

This major principle of preparation can be used to decrease the uncertainty and unpredictability of exams, thereby increasing both your self confidence and your luck. Anxiety increases in all performance situations, the more so the less certain you are about what will happen next. Conversely, the more certain you are of the future the greater your confidence.

WORK SMARTER NOT HARDER

UNKNOWN ———	KNOWN
You are uncertain	You are certain
You are anxious	You are confident

In the Exam Game uncertainty arises from not being sure of the questions which will appear on the exam paper. If a large proportion of your preparation is devoted to the questions which are likely to be asked, your confidence will increase substantially. One major task of your preparation is to move yourself as far to the right as possible. Put yourself into the shoes of the Examiner – what questions would you ask? What questions are asked?

THE EXPERIENCE OF JOHN – 'A' LEVEL STUDENT

John and I analysed the last five years Economics papers. One question had appeared 6 times in five years. "What do you think John" I asked. "Yes, it might come up again" he replied somewhat tentatively. "Not might John, IT WILL come up" I replied in slight exasperation.

Sure enough – the same question was asked on John's paper!

A STUDY IN PERFORMANCE PREPARATION

GRAHAM GOOCH'S ENGLAND TOUR OF THE WEST INDIES

In the Guardian (February 1990) Frank Keating reported on England's victory over cricket's world champions the West Indies. The two countries had played nineteen test matches and England had won none, until Graham Gooch was appointed as captain. His decision to prepare England properly for their 'performance', is an excellent example of meticulously planned preparation which resulted in victory for Gooch's team. 'Glory be, the whole thing looked from first to last to be actually presumed and planned for. Which believe it or not, it was . . .'

Whether or not you know anything about cricket, Frank Keating's article reflects importantly upon Gooch's determination to approach the matches differently from that of his predecessors. As the following extracts and comments make clear.

EXTRACT 1

From the moment Gooch put down the telephone in the autumn after being offered the job – knowing he was only first choice at the end of a calamitous chain of bitch and botch and blunder by those who play and, particularly, administer the senior game – he determined that if England were to go down yet again, then at least they would go down fighting. And fit.

Graham Gooch was four months away from his performance when he began his preparation. If you compare the similarity between your future exam performance and Graham Gooch's position, it should indicate how your own approach to preparation is to develop.

EXTRACT 2

Gooch, 37 this summer, first played Test cricket in 1975 – the year after England's last victory over the West Indians. Till yesterday he had played 19 unsuccessful games against the hitherto cruelly relentless world champions. Gooch took, as his vice-captain, just one from the old freemasonry – Allan Lamb, an enthusiast and fighter who has never turned up to 'go through the motions and though we'll probably lose, let's see what happens.'

Gooch and Lamb had collected 130 England caps between them, the other 14 players had only 65. But they were fresh, even innocent – and determined.

The majority of the general public probably thought that the only purpose of England touring, was to allow the West Indies an opportunity to play some brilliant cricket and record yet more outstanding victories. Whatever else Gooch and his vice captain Allan Lamb might have thought about their chances, they would have known and realized that their own confidence was fundamental to achieving success.

EXTRACT 3

If he had learned one thing from his previous and, for England, ignominious tours to the West Indies, it was that any ability to concentrate mentally for hours on end in sapping, tropical conditions derived directly from peak physical fitness.

'We can only do our very best,' said Gooch as they left Heathrow in January. 'If you see us doing our absolute utmost to the very best of our ability, it's all you can ask of us.'

To begin his preparation Graham Gooch knew that his own strengths and talents were decisive, he made the positive decision also to concentrate upon those things which would effect his performance.

EXTRACT 4

So once the touring team was selected this winter – with, to general consternation, almost all the old cabal and its prejudices and preconceptions either left out altogether or bribed to the Cape of No Hope – Gooch and the team manager, Mickey Stewart, organised a sustained series of long practice and fitness sessions at Headingley and Lilleshall for the party. To titters and snidery all round at such despairing stuff.

They even paid Geoffrey Boycott to examine and reorganise batting techniques – and Gooch himself spent hours in the nets with his canny, one time senior partner.

Maintaining his own personal development, Gooch then began to develop his team by determining an order of priority. The outcome of understanding what was required to be able to win against the West Indies, is best described by their captain Clive Lloyd's final accolade: 'A tremendously professional display . . . Gooch had done his homework . . . he knew exactly what to do.'

WHAT CAN YOU LEARN FROM THE GRAHAM GOOCH EXAMPLE?

1. 'IF YOU HAVE DONE YOUR HOMEWORK THE EXAM WILL BE A PIECE OF CAKE.

Successful performances are rarely accidental. They are always planned and prepared for, because there is a direct link between:

PREPARATION ⟶ PERFORMANCE ⟶ OUTCOME

2. ALL SUCCESSFUL PERFORMANCES BEGIN WITH YOURSELF

Knowledge about the kind of person you are, and about your behaviour both as a student and a performer in exams is required so that your programme of preparation can be planned, scheduled and controlled to culminate in a successful final performance.

3. YOU WILL PERFORM AS YOU PRACTISE

Preparation requires you to practise as you mean to perform – always practising the most important things, in precisely the right way.

4. SUSTAINED WORK WILL PAY OFF

Once a plan is decided, it must be implemented by well directed and sustained work.

5. PERFORMANCE PREPARATION PROGRAMMES ARE ABOUT DEVELOPMENT

Development occurs over a period of time, the logical outcome of positive decisions and a sustained system of behaviour. It doesn't matter what your talent and ability at the beginning, during preparation you will develop as a person – becoming more aware, more capable and more confident.

Development involves change: change requires a conscious decision by you that 'you want to change for the better' as well as honest and truthful self assessment to adjudge the starting point.

Your task is immensely easier than Gooch's. Examination performances are individual rather than team performances. No one is trying to stop you, or make it difficult for you to perform. Only you are involved in planning and controlling your development and performance programme.

THE PROGRAMME

THE PROGRAMME OF TOTAL PREPARATION EXPLAINED

STAGE 1: PLANNING

Used to lay the foundation of final performance. A student's route maps are decided and planned.

STAGE 2: ORGANISATION

Used to organise the details of the route map: resources, time, knowledge.

STAGE 3: FAMILIARISATION

Used to become familiar with all the elements of final performance: use of knowledge, use of time, practising exam performances, and to develop coping strategies.

STAGE 4: LEARNING

Used to commit the performance script to memory.

STAGE 5: PERFORMANCE

The Student performs in the exam room.

OVERALL OBJECTIVE

The programme's overall objective is personal development. By the time a student enters the exam room to begin their final performance, they will feel, not only more capable students, but more powerful and confident people.

THE PROCESS

The programme is designed to be cumulative, each stage building on its predecessor to increase, not only a student's ability but that ingredient vital to all performances – SELF-CONFIDENCE.

HOW LONG SHOULD YOU TAKE?

Only rough guidelines can be given in answer to this important question, because the needs, work patterns, lifestyles and commitments of students are so different.

If you are at school, college or university the formal timetable of the institution will organise – to a large extent – your programme and your time. If however you are working on your own, perhaps attached to colleges such as the Open University, Wolsey Hall or the National Extension College, there may be additional problems of integrating exam preparation with the other responsibilities and commitments of your life – work, family, children.

The timetable opposite is appropriate to "A" Level and first degree students. If your exams are at different times in the year it can easily be adapted to your needs.

A student should be open about receiving advice, but in the end, the time schedule chosen has to suit their own needs and way of life.

TIME-SCALE OF THE PROGRAMME					
STAGE	PLANNING STAGE	ORGANISATION STAGE	FAMILIARISATION STAGE	LEARNING STAGE	PERFORMING STAGE
START	Begin: 1st week March 12 weeks before	Begin: 3rd week March 9 weeks before	Begin: 3rd week April 6 weeks before	Begin: 3rd week May 2 weeks before	Begin: 2nd week June
DURATION	2/3 weeks	3/4 weeks	5 weeks	10/14 days	2/4 weeks

PACE AND INTENSITY

Students often think – indeed they are often told – that when they reach the revision part of their course, they must work "flat out". That is not so!

All performances, whatever the type, require performers to learn to control the pace at which they perform. There will be occasions when "flat out" pace and maximum intensity is required. There may even be short periods when a student works almost beyond their capabilities, but for the majority of the time, pace will be less than maximum. Exact measurement of intensity, particularly important when there is a need to change pace at different points in the programme, is impossible to give. The table below though is a guide.

CONTROL YOUR OWN PACE THROUGHOUT THE PROGRAMME: IT IS YOUR PACE THAT IS IMPORTANT (NOT YOUR PARENTS OR YOUR TEACHERS – WHATEVER THEY MAY SAY!)

CONTROL OF PACE AND INTENSITY

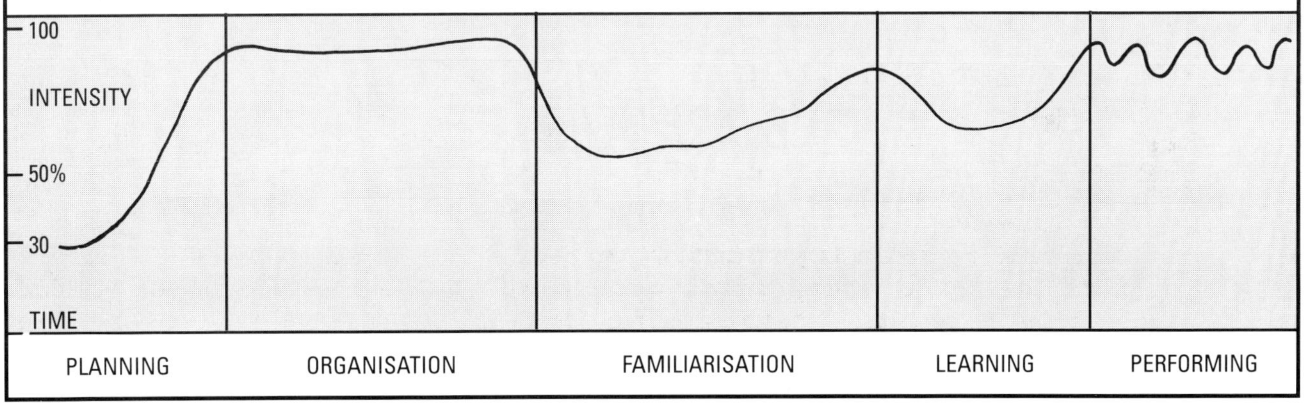

GUIDING PRINCIPLES

1. YOU are always the central focus: and YOU are always in control of your programme.
2. STAY IN THE PRESENT: the focus of your concentration should always be "what is happening NOW.
3. PROCEED BY SMALL STEPS: never rush or try to do too much. Always break tasks down and proceed one step at a time.
4. USE A ROUTE MAP: never proceed without knowing where you are going. Always plan your route map before you start work.

STAGE 1

PLANNING

STAGE 1 – PLANNING

THE PLANNING STAGE CONSIDERS – YOU !

"WHEREVER YOU ARE, IT IS THE PLACE TO START. WITH YOURSELF. THE EFFORT YOU EXPEND TODAY DOES MAKE A DIFFERENCE."

THE PERSON

- Learning about Yourself
- Self Confidence
- Self Concept
- How to improve your self concept
- How motivated are you?
- How to improve your motivation?
- Mental Rehearsal
- Anxiety
- Relaxation skills

THE STUDENT

- How do you learn best?
- How do you study best?
- Use of Learning Maps
- Your physical well-being
- What is the best environment in which to study?
- The skills of Time Management
- The importance of memory
- Concentration skills
- How to control your expectations and fear of failure

YOU: THE PERSON

LEARNING ABOUT YOURSELF

Understanding yourself as a person before you understand yourself as a student is important because, the attitudes, personal qualities and personality you possess already, play a crucial role in determining the effectiveness of your study skills.

The most critical factors determining the effective use of skills are your personality and your personal qualities – patience, care, deliberation, thoughtfulness, and control over the pace at which you work. Understanding yourself enhances your ability to control your performance and therefore your rate of success. The knowledge required to be successful is probably already part of you. Much of it is common sense. Most of it revolves around how you think and feel about yourself.

The programme centres on your self confidence. Students often say that when they enter the exam room, the feeling they most want to have is SELF CONFIDENCE. Self confidence is feeling in control of yourself and trusting your abilities and the situation. It does not occur easily or instantaneously. Developed over a period of time, it is the product of how we feel about ourselves and how others see us. To maintain your confidence at a good level all you have to do is to behave correctly etc . . .

HOW DO YOU FEEL ABOUT YOURSELF? DO YOU FEEL POSITIVE?

CONFIDENT PEOPLE KNOW THEY CAN, AND THEY DO

Self confidence is a factor in the formula for consistent high level performance. Much of what has been written about the development of a positive self concept applies to self confidence, one leads to the other. It could be argued that SELF CONFIDENCE is the base from which all success derives.

It involves a true and realistic expectation about achieving success. Self confidence is not concerned with what you HOPE to do, but with what you realistically EXPECT to do. As your self confidence increases, your performance will improve.

Self confidence is not elusive for you, what you have to do is to learn how to get onto the successful/self confidence spiral. Nearly all the mental skills dealt with in this book enable you to develop self confidence and maintain it.

HAVE YOU EVER NOTICED THAT WHEN YOU ARE FEELING GOOD ABOUT YOURSELF, OTHER PEOPLE ARE ALSO VERY NICE? ISN'T IT A SHAME THESE THINGS CHANGE?

Here are some key points to help you,

- try to put together a personal goalsetting programme which will help you to ensure that you achieve the goals you set yourself (for goalsetting see page 39).
- Make sure you complete the programme and not just the bits you find easy. You also have to deal with the bits which are uncomfortable and difficult.
- The key to becoming confident in yourself, and therefore successful, lies in working at the programme until have completed the task. Along the way some things may not work. Then you have to review the goals you've set yourself and try again. Learn from your experience and adjust.

If your expectations are at the right level you will set yourself realistic goals based on your ability. You should not attempt to set yourself unrealistic goals which are very difficult for you to achieve. Self confidence alone does not guarantee success, you also need the knowledge of the area being examined, and the skills and techniques to answer the questions. In order to succeed you need to set appropriate goals in all of these areas. No one becomes a success overnight. Be aware of your strengths and believe them. At the same time be aware of the areas which need more work and continue to work so that they also become strengths!

THE SUCCESS CYCLE

Follow the success cycle. Success begins with your positive self image which automatically leads to more self confidence. If the word 'negative' is substituted for 'positive' the cycle works in reverse. Follow it around and see what happens to your success!

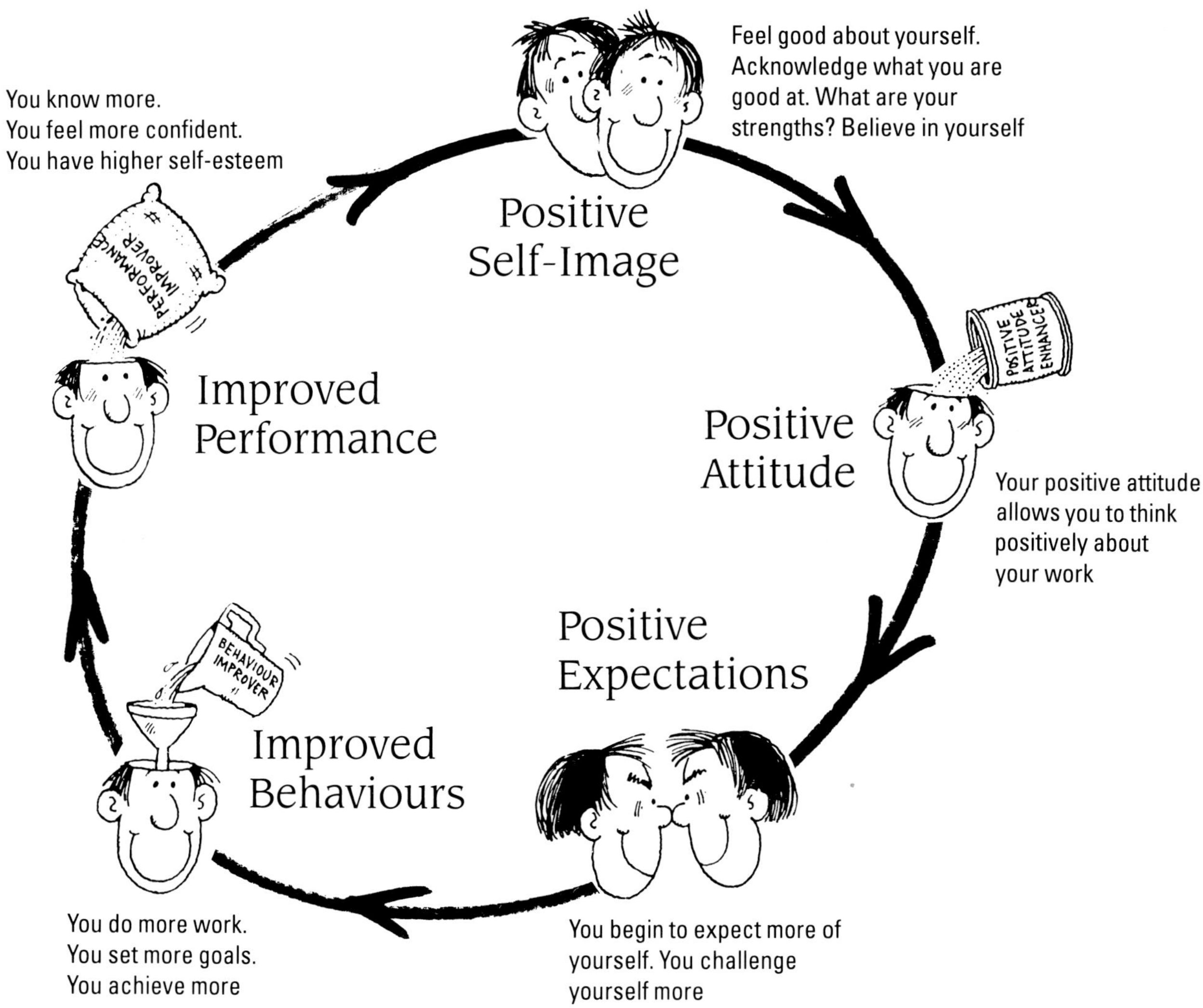

What kind of words help you to feel confident?
What are the components of your notions of confidence?
List all the factors that contribute to your feeling of confidence.

______________________	______________________
______________________	______________________
______________________	______________________
______________________	______________________
______________________	______________________
______________________	______________________
______________________	______________________
______________________	______________________

Use this list of words as your confidence formula. Use it, carry it with you, say it to yourself (This may be different for different subjects).

SELF CONCEPT

The world in which you live is a reflection of yourself. When you loathe yourself, you loathe everybody else. When you enjoy being who you are, the rest of the world is wonderful. Your self concept is the picture you have of yourself. This picture is 'coloured' by the thoughts you have about yourself and other people's reactions to you. The kind of experiences and your success and failure at the things you have attempted will also determine how you picture yourself.

Because you believe the picture you have of yourself to be fact, you will proceed to behave and live within the boundary of this self picture. The picture you have of yourself therefore determines,

EVERYTHING YOU DO, YOUR THOUGHTS AND ACTIONS STEM FROM THE WAY YOU SEE YOURSELF.

- How much you enjoy and like the world in which you live.
- The degree to which you will succeed and what you will accomplish in life.

Do any of the following sound like you? Are these the kind of things you're saying to yourself?

- I'm not very good at maths!
- I'm hopeless at art!
- I've always been a donkey at ball games!
- I'm too fat to wear mini-skirts!
- I won't do very well I'm not clever enough!

Let's explore the maths example a little further.

If you see yourself as being poor at maths, you will always have some difficulties with numbers. This could have been caused by an early bad experience at school, that has helped you to develop an attitude that says, 'Whatever I do, I can't do maths.' Consequently you don't try! You probably tell everyone else that you are no good at maths! You fall further and further behind in class work and homework. You will then say, 'I told you I was hopeless.' If there should ever be a time when you do succeed in some area of maths you will only think that it's a fluke! The more you tell others that you can't do maths, the more you believe it, and the more embedded your self picture becomes. You will not be very good at maths.

ARE THERE SOME AREAS WHICH MAKE YOU 'FEEL GOOD ABOUT YOURSELF'. IF SO HANG ONTO THEM, YOU NEED THEM.

WHO AM I?

Discover how you feel about yourself at the moment. Do this simple exercise. Write 10 statements in the space provided about who you are. e.g. *I am 5'5" tall (objective),* Ask yourself the question several times before writing down the things which come into your head.

WHAT ARE THE AREAS WHICH MAKE YOU FEEL NOT QUITE SO CONFIDENT ABOUT YOURSELF (WRITE THEM DOWN).

Now try to write 10 statements about how you feel about yourself. These statements will be about your emotions, abilities, personality, e.g. I get angry very quickly. Now try to write down how you think other people see. you. Do you think they see you as, lazy, inefficient, good time guy/gal, serious, hardworking, a trier, talented, works only when has to. Be very objective and have a look at what kind of picture you have of yourself at the moment.

OBJECTIVE	EMOTIONAL	HOW OTHERS VIEW ME

Is the mental picture of yourself either:

POSITIVE →
or
NEGATIVE →

STEPS TO IMPROVE THE PICTURE OF YOURSELF

Step 1
Know yourself well enough to recognise the things which need some help and improvement. Recognise and give yourself a pat on the back, for the things which are O.K. (If you have done the above exercises thoroughly and honestly then you will be well on the way to fulfilling step number 1).

Step 2
Begin trying to change the way you think and talk to yourself about yourself. Keep reminding yourself about the positive things you believe about yourself, and begin LISTENING to the things which you are telling yourself which are negative. Tell yourself to say STOP and try to turn the negative statements into positives. (You will get further guidance about this process from the section on Self talk and Affirmations on page 33).

TO REALLY BELIEVE IN YOURSELF:
HEAR IT
WRITE IT DOWN
SEE IT
SAY IT TO YOURSELF
BELIEVE IT
BECOME IT

Step 3
Start LISTENING to what other people are saying to you. Remember the good and positive things, write them down and begin saying them to yourself.

Note very carefully the not so good and negative things being said to you. Always try to change these negative statements into positive ones and begin saying them to yourself.

Try to see yourself as a dynamic entity. It changes according to how you view yourself, how other people see you, and the experiences you have. But you tend to operate within a range of behaviour. For example, perhaps you are the kind of person who is only happy for 50% of the time. Whenever things are going extra well you may think: 'Things are not meant to be this good for this long, something is bound to go wrong.' Then of course it does go wrong and you say 'I knew it couldn't last!'

You will create your own quality of life, and this will be based on what kind of picture you have of yourself. Well, what's it going to be? Are you going to control your own performance, because if you are, this is where it starts, with you!

SELF ENHANCEMENT SKILLS

Try some of the following 'self enhancement skills' to help you to become a positive, self confident person.

SELF TALK
One of the most useful skills to help you to keep a positive picture of yourself is self talk. Self talk can be described as those words or phrases which you say to yourself, about yourself. It is important because it influences how you view yourself and your situations, and because of the important effect it has on your level of performance. Your words and thoughts affect your circumstances and they also determine your experiences and attract particular kinds of comment from other people.

"THE MOST IMPORTANT THINGS EVER SAID TO US ARE SAID BY OUR INNER SELVES."
ADELAIDE BRY

SELF TALK is the switch, which either switches on or switches off, the way you approach a performance. The more you understand and learn to apply self talk properly the better the effect on your exam performance.

WHAT YOU SAY, IS WHAT YOU GET

How often in the past have you said to yourself,

"There's no way I can pass this exam."

"I hope I don't make a mess of my chemistry experiment today, I usually do."

"I hope I remember my lines without prompting, my mind usually goes blank".

Therefore it comes as little surprise to you when you don't pass the exam, when you do make a mess of the experiment or when you do 'dry up' and have to be prompted. You may not realise it but your SELF TALK had a lot to do with the nature of the performance.

YOU ARE THE ONLY PERSON IN CHARGE OF YOUR MOUTH.
ONLY OPEN YOUR MOUTH WHEN YOU HAVE SOMETHING POSITIVE TO SAY.

When you become very serious about your exam performance you should only speak when you are feeling POSITIVE and you should think carefully before you begin to run yourself DOWN.

The importance of 'self talk' in determining your attitude is illustrated in this diagram:

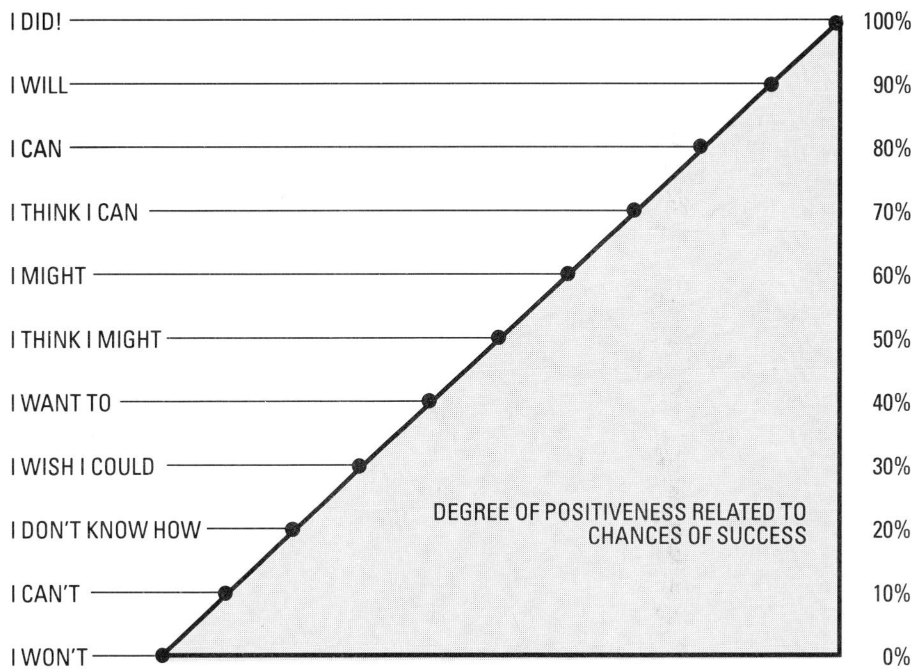

SELF TALK is a conscious thing. You know you're saying things to yourself. Do you consciously talk yourself down and out of things therefore destroying your self confidence?

OR

Do you consciously talk yourself into performing well and therefore building up your own self confidence?

There are 2 kinds of self talk. – POSITIVE – NEGATIVE

Let's first look at NEGATIVE SELF TALK.
Negative self talk varies from just worrying about something, to becoming extremely anxious and feeling terrified.

LOW worried distracted	⟵⟶	HIGH anxiety attacks terror

All negative self talk on the continuum sets the stage for a poor performance. Worrying to one degree of another is probably the place where most of you see yourself. These are some common examples of such performance worries.

- I haven't done enough preparation
- I wish I'd taken this exam more seriously
- I didn't understand that in the lesson, so I've no chance in the exam
- I just can't get myself organised.
- 'I've got butterflies in my stomach and I feel sick.'
- 'My hands are shaking so badly I can hardly write.'
- 'That noise is driving me mad, and I can't think clearly.'
- 'I can't work in this room, it's too dark.'
- 'Everybody, except me, seems to be able to do this.'
- 'The rest of my Physics group seem much brighter than I am.'
- 'If I don't do well enough in these exams I will '

  'lose my place at university'

  'upset and disappoint my parents'

These are all negative put-downs which you may say to yourself, or you've heard other people say to or about themselves. Such negative statements reflect worry about the negative consequences of a future performance. If you allow yourself to become aware of negative feelings and say such negative things to yourself it will reinforce pessimistic attitudes, low self esteem and a tendency to give up.

KUBISTANT. (1986)
YOU . . . MAY NOT BE ABLE TO JUMP OVER A TALL BUILDING IN A SINGLE BOUND – YET! BUT IF YOU CONSTANTLY SAY TO YOURSELF THAT THERE IS NO WAY IN THE WORLD THAT I CAN EVER REACH THE TOP OF THAT BUILDING, YOU WILL NEVER FIND THE STAIRCASE."

WHERE DO YOU FALL ON THIS NEGATIVE SELF TALK CONTINUUM?

POSITIVE SELF TALK OR AFFIRMATIONS

One of the reasons why negative self talk has such power over you is that you have probably been saying such things to yourself for a long time, without being aware of it. It has become a habit. The mind then seeks to confirm the negative talk, and you behave in a negative way.

Step 1

In order to transform your negative talk into positive talk you must first:
- Begin by listening to the positive things you're saying to yourself.
- Become aware of any 'put-downs' you're saying to yourself.

Step 2
Decide a length of time (one week would be ideal, but if you can't manage that, two or three days will do) when you will try to become totally aware of your negative talk.

WRITE DOWN THE POSITIVE THINGS, AND THE 'PUT-DOWNS'.

Step 3
Now that you are more aware of some of the 'put downs' you have been using, continue to monitor the negative talk, but from now on, when you catch yourself talking negatively:

- Challenge it, by saying 'stop, that's stupid.'
- Then re-phrase the negative by making it into a positive phrase.
- Make the positive phrase as simple, direct and as positive as possible.

Let's imagine that you keep putting yourself down about your ability to cope with algebra. The negative statements may sound something like,

- I'm really hopeless at this subject.
- No matter how I work at it I never get it right.

NOW REPHRASE THEM IN A POSITIVE WAY.

- I'm beginning to learn more about this subject.
- I'm doing the best I can.
- I'm well prepared in algebra.
- I'm going to enjoy doing my algebra.

This is the process of turning those negative put-downs into positive statements.

It's a game you can play, because the more you become aware of the put-downs, the more you weaken their power over you.

THE A.C.R. PROCESS

Ⓐ Awareness of negative self talk.

Ⓒ Challenge the negative self talk.

Ⓡ Redefine and make positive

Above all believe what you are saying.

What you are doing by using positive self talk is simply AFFIRMING or CONFIRMING what you believe about your qualities as a person, the skills you have and the attributes which you bring to the situation.

All high level performers whether they are sportsmen/women, opera stars business men or musicians use such AFFIRMATIONS to help remind them of their positive performance strengths.

There are 3 types of self talk or affirmation

1. BASIC – very general, positive self talk.

I am relaxed.
I enjoy what I can do.
I am proud of what I do.
I trust myself.

YOU ARE NOT SHOWING OFF OR BOASTING, YOU ARE SIMPLY REINFORCING WHAT YOU BELIEVE.

Fill in some which apply to you

1. ____________________ 4. ____________________

2. ____________________ 5. ____________________

3. ____________________ 6. ____________________

2. ACTIVITY/SKILL – tell yourself about your skills.

I am a relaxed swimmer.
I am a graceful dancer.

Fill in some which apply to you.

1. ____________________ 4. ____________________

2. ____________________ 5. ____________________

3. ____________________ 6. ____________________

3. PROCESS – positive words which you may say to yourself during a performance

Go for it.	Concentrate.
I'm ready.	Easy.
I'm prepared.	Good.
Softly.	Relax.
Focus.	

Fill in some you may use before or during your performance in the exam.

1. ____________________ 4. ____________________

2. ____________________ 5. ____________________

3. ____________________ 6. ____________________

Positive self talk or affirmations do work and you can make them effective and powerful for you.

Here is a reminder of the process through which you go to help you to discover and develop the new positive you.

1. Listen and become aware of your own put-downs.
2. List put-downs. Continue to discover and monitor them.
3. Challenge them. Begin to try redefining them.
4. Believe and re-construct your affirmations as positively as possible.
5. Always construct affirmations in PRESENT TENSE.
6. Constantly repeat affirmations. Build on them and believe them.

FOR EVERY OUTSTANDING PERFORMANCE OR ACHIEVEMENT BOTH SELF DISCIPLINE AND PERSISTENCE ARE COMMON FACTORS.

Now that you are beginning to understand yourself a little better and you are also feeling more positive about things, you need to consider two very important factors. Self discipline and motivation are essential elements for everyone, no matter how talented you are. Consistently good high level performance is never determined by talent or ability alone. Persistence is the ability to stick to your resolution long after the mood and enthusiasm in which you made the resolution has passed.

1. Are you a quitter or do you have the self discipline and persistence to continue to work hard at your revision programme?

2. How motivated are you to do well and achieve the best you can? Why are you doing all this work?

MOTIVATION

Motivation is the drive and energy you have which keeps you wanting to go on doing what you're doing and achieving the performance standards and expectations which you have set yourself.

Consistent high level performance =

Talent & Ability X **Motivation** X **Self Confidence** X **Self Discipline & Persistence**

HOW MOTIVATED ARE YOU

THERE ARE:
4 TYPES OF PEOPLE
THOSE WHO WATCH THINGS HAPPEN
THOSE TO WHOM THINGS HAPPEN
THOSE WHO DON'T KNOW WHAT HAPPENS
THOSE WHO MAKE THINGS HAPPEN

Everyone talks about being motivated. Motivated to do things, motivated to achieve certain standards, motivated to go on working at something even though it is going badly, motivated to do as well as they possibly can within their own ability. What is motivating you to go on working at your revision, when you could be doing something else? The reasons can be very varied.

- You have to, because your parents and school are saying you have to?
- You want to get into a particular University and you require grades?
- In the future you want to pursue a particular career and that means in order to get the job with the 'accountancy' firm you need to prove that you have had a good sound education especially in relevant subjects?
- You are good at taking exams, and that makes you feel good. Like you have really achieved something?

- You can do it because you thoroughly enjoy the challenge offered to you – through the planning, learning and execution of your skills. It's an achievement?

Motivation is clearly an important ingredient in your planning and eventual exam performance. Its impact has an importance in everything you do, not only for your exam preparation. Without motivation you would live a very dull life indeed.

YOU DO NEED TO KNOW WHY YOU ARE DOING THIS WORK. WHAT IS DRIVING YOU OR WHAT NEEDS ARE YOU FULFILLING.

Are you motivated because,

- **You enjoy the challenge**

The feelings of excitement are important to you, while others require less stimulation to keep them happy.

- **Your need to feel competent at what you do?**

You need to experience some success and to feel that you are at least good at something. In fact you are a much better person simply because you have achieved something. Depending on your experiences at school, or in past exam performances, you will already tend to be a winning thinker or a losing thinker.

Winning thinker =
You have experienced some success in the past and done quite well. You believe that you have the ability to do well. This inspires confidence and you go on being successful You will probably direct your energies to the challenge that the work and the exam offers you. You will feel pleased with yourself when you do well, but will also accept the responsibility should something not work out right.

Losing thinker =
You have experienced some failures in the past, and are consequently full of self-doubt and anxiety. You probably think that you don't have the ability to do well. If you have had some success, you probably feel that it was a stroke of luck. The questions were easy, you had an on day, the teacher was feeling kind when he/she marked the papers, and so on! You will blame yourself for your failures and yet take very little credit for your successes. You will be very well armed with your excuses for poor results, and performances. 'I didn't feel so well.' 'My pen ran out, and I couldn't get the other one to work properly'. 'Well, that teacher never has liked me, no matter how hard I try, it doesn't matter.'

HELP YOURSELF TO BECOME AND STAY MOTIVATED.

MOTIVATION STRATEGY 1: PERSONAL CONTRACTS

Let's suppose that one of your subjects causes you to feel constantly low and unmotivated to get on with the work. Drawing up a personal contract with yourself regarding the work may be one answer to your problems. This works for some people, because they feel they have a duty to themselves, and therefore a responsibility to fulfill the contract. Get your teacher, parents or a close friend to witness the contract, and then place it in a position where you are always reminded of it, in bedroom, kitchen, inside note books, everywhere you will be able to see it. This way you will frequently be reminded of the contract to yourself. It's your responsibility!

Example A

> I, the undersigned, promise myself that I will work for 2 hours a day for the week beginning, March 4th-11th on my physics revision. I will do it preferably in the morning and BEFORE I do any other revision.
>
> Signed ____________________
>
> Witnessed ____________________

Example B

> I, ____________________ promise that I will begin my revision daily at 10am. and continue until 12.30pm. Begin again at 2pm and continue until 5.30pm. I will do this until I have managed to get to the Learning stage in all 3 of my A level subjects.
> I will begin this on March 29th.
>
> Signed ____________________
>
> Witnessed ____________________

You may feel that you would like to make more short term contracts with yourself. That's O.K. It is very important that you do fulfil your obligations to the contract set. Remain realistic, and every contract you fulfil will make you feel a sense of achievement. In the end you will enjoy the process so much that you begin to look forward to fulfilling a contract and making another.

MOTIVATION STRATEGY: 2
HAVING A CHANGE AND REWARDING YOURSELF.
This strategy involves having a change of focus, environment and task. You may often feel stale and bored by working at revision so long. If you do, have a complete change. Go and do something completely different – play tennis, listen to your favourite group, hire a video, paint a picture, join your friends and go out for a meal. The saying 'a change is as good as a rest' does work to some extent because when you come back to the work you feel refreshed and more able to work with a purpose.

What you must not do is feel guilty about having a change. Give yourself permission to do this, make it a reward for all the hard work you have put in and will continue to put in. Quality of work is important not the quantity! So reward yourself, you're allowed.

MOTIVATION STRATEGY 3: GOALSETTING
This is one of the best ways to remain motivated in your work. Goal setting is about knowing what you want to achieve, and telling yourself how well you intend to do it. Goals require planning, but this strategy will help you to focus on the particular activity you are doing and you will also know just how much

effort you will have to put in to achieve the intended outcome. Once achieved you will feel a real sense of achievement.

Your mind is a little bit like an iceberg. The area above the water is your conscious mind and tends to express itself in a very logical way. However, the bigger piece, below the water, is your subconscious mind. This deals with how you feel about what you're doing or how you feel about yourself.

This is how it works.

Conscious mind –
'I really should be doing some extra work on my Physics.'

Subconscious mind –
'I hate physics and I'm not very good at it.'

Conscious mind –
'I understand the meaning of these formulae.'

Subconscious mind –
'I feel so pleased with myself. I'm really confident about my work now.

When there is a conflict between the two minds it hinders your success. The secret is therefore to make them united. Success means that what you say logically you want, and is also what you feel you want to do. On the whole the brain tends to react more readily to an emotional feeling rather than to the logicality of thought. But try to stay with the logicality.

The time goals take to complete can be within the same day, a week, a month or by the end of the revision period, and during the exam period itself. This depends on you.

GOALS ARE NOT ONLY FOR THE PEOPLE WHO CAN DO IT! THEY ARE FOR EVERYONE!

Here are some of the benefits of goalsetting.
a. Goals help to monitor your progress and therefore keep you on your route map and maintain your self-confidence because of the progress being made.
b. Goals allow for progressive achievement, and the completion of tasks. This ensures a feeling of well-being. 'Good, I've done that, and that . . . It's a good feeling. They keep you motivated.

Examples:

- Learning 3 or 4 mathematical formulae and their application, completing six example questions which utilise this knowledge.
- Learning to précis a particular part of a set novel.
- Reviewing where you are in relation to your whole programme.

Kinds of goals to set
There are two major kinds of goals for you to set.

1. Outcome goals
An outcome goal is what you want to achieve in the end. e.g. wanting to pass the exam and achieve at least a grade C; wanting to win a game of tennis.
Passing and winning become the outcome of your achievements. Whilst outcomes are important they DO NOT help you to achieve your goal.

GOALSETTING HAS INFLUENCED THE PERFORMANCE OF PEOPLE AT ALL LEVELS AND HELPED THEIR CONFIDENCE TO REMAIN HIGH AND THEIR MOTIVATION TO REMAIN POSITIVE.

2. Performance goals

Performance goals help you to plan how you will achieve the final outcome. These become the route by which you reach your outcome goal.

Just by setting your own goals will not automatically improve your performance. You have to:

- Make sure they are appropriate for you
- Keep reviewing and evaluating them

They may need amending. You may be achieving more than you thought you would!

When you have achieved all the performance goals at each stage, the outcome is more likely to be exactly as you planned. Use the following guidelines to help you to prepare a goal-setting programme. Try it for just one of your areas of work to start with.

'GROW' EXERCISE:
Step 1: G = The Goal
What do you want to achieve?

Look at your priorities and the areas which may need work in the first instance. Set very specific goals. 'To try my best' isn't good enough, and will not be effective. BUT 'Work at Act 1 of the Tempest with a view to understanding,

- The plot
- The characters

will be much more effective. Be as precise as possible.

Step 2: R = Reality
Where are you now in relation to the goals you wish to achieve? Be very honest with yourself. How much work has to be done? How important is this area of work for you? Where are you NOW?

Check your strengths and areas which need more work and the resulting priorities. Check your time management log and work out precisely how much time is available to you in the months, weeks, hours left to you.

(Refer to P58 for work in Time Management)

Step 3: O = Options.
What courses of action are open to you?

For example you could,
- Spend more time with the subject.
- Make sure that there are no distractions. (Time robbers. P?)
- Make sure the relevant material is available.
- Dismiss the whole area, it's not important.

Step 4: W = Wrap up
How much time will you commit to this goal?

Make a decision based on priorities.
What kind of support will you need if you are to succeed in achieving your goal? eg. Help from the librarian; help from the teachers in terms of further explanation; parental help in understanding what you're trying to do this afternoon; therefore is it possible to have my meal later today?
When will you start? You will begin TODAY!

(Adapted from the model used by Hemery & Whitmore. 1989)

If you follow this process it will help you to establish goals.

TO BE EFFECTIVE, GOALS SHOULD BE:

1. **Specific.**
2. **Time related,** (always be specific about time – in the next hour, I will do . . . by the end of the week I will have finished . . etc).
3. **Self controlled and personal,** (they are yours to control).
4. **Challenging yet achievable,** (don't set them too high, which you cannot achieve, or too simple so that they are too easily reached. Make sure you have to achieve them with work).
5. **Set performance goals rather than outcome goals,** (you can't control the outcome, but you can control the performance – the way you get to the outcome).
6. **Measurable,** (try to set the goal in such a way that it is measurable. eg. I will attempt 6 small questions this week in relation to the History paper. By the end of next week I will have read through all my work on Chaucer and organised it into revisable parts.)
7. **Flexible,** (goals are not cast in stone. They can be altered. If after evaluation you feel they need amending, then do it. Periodic evaluation should occur if your goals are to remain challenging and achievable).

Now you have enough information to begin establishing a goal-setting programme for yourself. If you can discuss your goal-setting programme with a teacher, or share it with a friend, or understanding parents you may find it easier in the first instance. Use one of the examples of goalsetting forms in the appendix for this work. Or you can devise one for yourself.

ALL GOALS SHOULD BE POSITIVE

MOTIVATION STRATEGY 4: IMAGERY
Imagery is the ability to produce mental pictures or images which originate in your imagination. Everyone thinks in pictures. You use your mind's eye to see quite clearly pictures or images of yourself doing all kinds of things. It may be seeing yourself as a very good tennis player, or a successful pianist, or even a successful exam candidate!

When you use your imagination, you use all your senses.

The word LEMON, may evoke an image of something that is bright yellow and there is a bitter taste. You may also see the letters L E M O N.

In this example
the senses of sight and taste are being used.

The word BELL, may evoke an image of small bells swinging from side to side or one large bell swinging. You may in the first instance, hear the sound of the bells, and you may also see the word B E L L.

In this example
the senses of sight and sound are being used.

A picture can be worth many words. The more you use all your senses to create a 'mind picture' the more easily you will learn your material. (Check what has been said in this book about, the different ways in which people learn, and your 7 intelligences).

Once you become good at this skill you will find yourself retaining and recalling material easily and the material is there instantly. There are basically two ways of using imagery or visualisation:

1. **You can watch yourself as on the video.** In other words you are outside watching. e.g. you can watch yourselves in the exam room, watch yourself writing good clear and successful answers, watch yourself playing tennis, watch yourself as you go for an invigorating walk. This is viewing the scene in a detached way.

2. **You can also see yourself as if you are actually there in the situation.** You can actually feel yourself sitting in the seat in the exam room. When you look up it is as if you are in the room looking at the clock at the front of the room, seeing the girl's hair and blue sweater in front of you, you hear the rustle of papers, and the sighs of the people around as they turn over their papers. This is viewing the scene as a much fuller experience. It is as if you are there.

This means that more senses are being used. The main senses to develop are, sight, feeling in the muscles, touch, hearing and smell. Both methods are legitimate, but the more of your senses you can use the better will be the experience for you. If you can 'be there' in your imagination then you have more chance of combining the logical sense of knowing the subject with the recognition of how good the feelings are attached to it.

Try the following exercise
Think back to an event which was important for you. It could be something to do with your musical talent, sporting talent, or just a special event such as attending a wedding.

1. Try to recreate the event as an observer, in a detached way.
2. Try to recreate the event as if you are there seeing it once again through your own eyes.
Notice the difference. Keep practising by using all kinds of different events.

Follow these useful guidelines when practising your imagery.

- Start by feeling relaxed.
- Stay alert and become focused. (both relaxation and concentration are needed to use imagery successfully. The image and the signals become stronger with concentration).
- Use the present tense. In other words, be there NOW. Take in as much detail as you can.
- Try to use all the senses.
- Try to use the imagery at the correct speed.
- Practise the skill regularly. It is much better to do 10-15 minutes daily at certain times of the day than to do 50 minutes on one day a week.
- Enjoy it. – The more you enjoy your pictures the more you will enjoy the actual performance. If you are not enjoying the picture you're getting then you should stop and do something else.
- All of your picture and images, should depict you being successful. If at any time you see yourself being unsuccessful then stop and do something else.

THIS CAN BE A POWERFUL SKILL. YOU GET IN PERFORMANCE WHAT YOU SEE. (IF YOU SLOW DOWN THE WAY YOU ANSWER QUESTIONS, OR THE WAY YOU WRITE THEM THAT IS LIKELY TO HAPPEN IN THE EXAM).

Everyone has the ability to use their imagination, it just needs some practise. Try some of the following exercises just to prove to yourself that you can imagine things. Then try to understand which sense is being used.

- Imagine biting into a lemon.
- Imagine yourself listening to bells ringing.
- Imagine the feeling of the hot sun on your back.

Create this scene for yourself;
There is a bonfire burning somewhere in the neighbourhood. See the smoke rising and the flames creeping up from the bottom. See the bonfire as large or small and try to smell the burning leaves and wood which has been on the fire.

Did you get an image. Did you see the colour, smell the burning. Watch the smoke curling and swirling about. Could you see the colour of the flames, and watch them lick around the logs and leaves. Were you there? You could not have answered any of these questions if you were not capable of creating a picture for yourself in your imagination.

You can also imagine anything to do with your revision.

YOU GET WHAT YOU SEE. SEE YOURSELF AS SUCCESSFUL AND THE CHANCES ARE YOU WILL BE. YOU WILL AT LEAST GIVE YOURSELF A BETTER CHANCE OF BEING SUCCESSFUL.

English Literature – create a picture of the characters you are reading about. What kinds of things would they have worn. What kind of feelings and emotions did they have in the context of the book or poem.

Mathematics – create a picture of a formula, create a debate between you and another person, explaining the meaning of the formula and how it is applied.

History – this is a lot like the skill you have already used in English Literature. You could actually see a movie of the things which you are learning about or build a screen of pictures which you could also write down and look at.

You should try to think about the areas you are studying and apply the skills of imagery. Tap all your resources, the senses. Seeing, hearing, touching, smelling and feeling. Explore the who, where, when, what and why in relation to the subjects you are working at. This makes it fun.

This is also a helpful skill to help you to remain motivated. Use all the imagery skills you have learnt for your subjects on yourself.

See yourself as being successful, and be there being successful.

MENTAL REHEARSAL

This is the use of Imagery as a routine immediately before an examination. It is helpful for you to go through a PRE-EXAM imagery routine BEFORE EVERY EXAM. The routine should be your own and should be practised before you try to use it before the exam.

It is a simple, but very effective skill using the skills you have already gained from your work in imagery. It involves running through a successful attempt of an answer or part of an answer on an exam paper in your mind immediately before performing in the exam. For example if there is an area of the paper which you are not quite certain of, then you can plan a very good answer and keep seeing yourself answering successfully on the paper, in the way that you have planned.

This kind of process helps you to remove the doubt that you have about an area of work, a skill and will help you to 'fine tune' the brain, mind and body ready for you to act in the exam.

Follow these simple procedures to help you develop a pre-exam routine for mental rehearsal.

1. Spend a few minutes relaxing before you begin. You may lie down or sit comfortably. Allow any tension to dissolve from your body.
2. When you feel sufficiently relaxed, begin to create a picture in your mind's eye of yourself walking into the exam room, sitting down at the desk, turning over the paper, reading it, and quietly preparing to answer the questions selected.
3. Try to re-create vividly the picture in great detail. The noises in the room, see yourself and what you are wearing, feel the temperature, feel the muscles picking up the pen, or turning over the pages, and any tastes, feelings and accompanying smells.
4. Once you have created the scene, then you can commence answering the

paper, or part of the paper. As you repeat this picture make sure that you pay particular attention to how you are feeling and how well you are performing. Try to see and feel yourself performing better every time you go through the sequence.

5. Set yourself a number of attempts at one time, perhaps 10 or 20 to begin with. Make sure that every time you see yourself, you are being successful. If at any time it does not feel successful, then you must stop the mental rehearsal and go and do something else. You only have time for being successful.
6. If at any time you can follow the mental rehearsal with the actual physical practice of writing an answer it will help your performance.

ARE YOU FEELING ANXIOUS?

When people know in advance that a performance is required they often begin to feel a little nervous. They say 'I've a feeling of butterflies in my stomach.' This is quite natural. You do need to have some feeling of excitement if you are going to perform well.

Do you know whether you are naturally an anxious person? For example, do you have feelings of worry, fear, apprehension or tension about different areas of your life and your forthcoming exams? These feelings are very similar to the feelings of stress and if they are very noticeable and you constantly have the deep hollow feeling in your stomach then they can be dangerous. Unless you learn to control them, they may affect anything you try to do. In other words they lessen your chances of giving a good performance, whether it is giving a speech, taking a driving test, or doing a physics exam. Understanding the feeling of stress is a good starting point. Once you understand it, and recognise it, then you give yourself a better chance of controlling it, before it affects your performance.

STRESS IS NOT IMPOSED BY OTHER PEOPLE. YOU IMPOSE IT ON YOURSELF. OTHER PEOPLE AND EVENTS MAY CONTRIBUTE TO IT, BUT IT IS ALWAYS UTLIMATELY UNDER YOUR OWN CONTROL.

For instance when there are too many activities going on in your life, or when too many unexpected things happen, stress levels increase and control becomes difficult.

If you can remember that the level of stress is ultimately under your control, and you can say 'no', then you will automatically lower the level of stress you are feeling.

Stress is often caused by people worrying about something which is quite outside their control, for example:

a) when people are caught in a traffic jam which might make them late for an appointment, they fret and work themselves into a temper.

CONTROL IS IMPORTANT

b) when you are trying to do too many things at once, you may try to increase time, by sleeping less and working longer.

You cannot control the traffic jam, relax and stay in the present. You cannot control the demands which other people sometimes make of you, but you can control your own use of time. Reorganise and reschedule your time more effectively.

Exercise 1

On a sheet of paper list all the things which you are feeling anxious about at the moment, in any area of your life: school, social, sports, exams.

Go down the list and tick the ones which you cannot control. – Then forget them. – YOU CAN'T DO ANYTHING ABOUT THEM!

Look at the items which are in your control. Decide what is causing the problem. In other words, why are you feeling stressed about them at the moment?

Keep the list, because the next section will help you to learn how to deal with the problems which you have.

Managing your stress

Stress is an imbalance between what is perceived as being demanded of you in a particular situation. eg. making a speech, doing an exam, or taking the driving test, and how you feel about your capabilities in order to achieve what is being demanded.

As a student you are aware of what you have to learn and know, in order to pass the exam at the appropriate level for your needs, BUT you believe that you are not capable of reaching the level expected. The difference between the two causes anxiety and therefore you feel stressed.

A and **B** need to be kept in balance. Like this:

Stress is being managed and is under control. The performance has a chance of succeeding.

Stress not being coped with. Less chance of success.

Exercise 2.

How do you know you're stressed?
Answer the following questions by ticking YES or NO.

	YES	NO
1. Do you find it difficult to concentrate and are easily distracted?	☐	☐
2. Is your memory not working as well as it should, and you respond to the questions much more slowly than usual?	☐	☐
3. Do you tend to make more mistakes than you would under normal circumstances?	☐	☐
4. Does your organisation and planning tend to be poor?	☐	☐
5. Do you become confused, irrational, and your critical powers between reality and objectivity become confused?	☐	☐
6. Do you worry, feel that everything is hopeless and you feel depressed?	☐	☐
7. You don't feel very good about yourself as a person? (I'm hopeless!)	☐	☐
8. You motivation decreases, you don't really want to do it, you feel tired all the time, are not sleeping well and miss sessions which may be important?	☐	☐

Recognise your symptoms. A YES is a symptom of stress.

Stress proof yourself.
Don't allow the stress to ruin your exams, don't hope that it will go away, it won't, but you can do something about it.

The first step of learning to deal with stress is recognising your own symptoms. You will not have all the symptoms, some will be easier to recognize than others.

Emotions can be positive or negative. They can inspire your exam performance or they can inhibit your performance.

You do need some level of excitement to perform well. Consequently, you need to know how much is enough for you. You need just the right amount for you without feeling tense and therefore feeling greatly stressed.

If you need help to cope with exam stress, try some of the following skills, all of which are outlined in this book.

a) Relaxation skills.

b) Goalsetting skills.

c) Positive self talk skills.

d) Imagery skills. – see yourself as being relaxed and in control

e) Time management skills.

Be aware that the following elements can assist your control of stress.

a) Eating and drinking well and regularly.

b) Physical work of some kind. (walking, tennis, swimming, jogging, fitness programmes and weights).

c) Trying to get enough sleep.

d) Managing your time in an efficient way.

(Check the physical needs during exams and time management sections).

Practise recognising your own symptoms then apply the appropriate technique. Don't wait until the stress reaches a high level. As soon as you recognise the feeling whether bodily, mentally or your behaviour changes, just use the appropriate technique to help you to control your performance. It will take time to work, so keep practising it!

One other method of dealing with stress is self pep talks.

For example,

Pep talk for lowering stress

Select a few short phrases or key words which will help you to deal with your stress, e.g. 'Slow it down', 'Breathe', 'Relax, breathe, take it easy'. 'I feel loose and relaxed, breathe.'

Pep talk for lifting excitement level

Select a few short phrased or key words which will help you to lift your level of excitement. e.g. 'I'm well prepared, I can do this'. 'This is my exam, nobody elses, and I'm ready for it'. 'Come on, this is what all the hard work has been for'. 'This is fun, I'm really going to enjoy this'.

When you have your own phrases or words, write them down on a small card and keep repeating them to yourself.

RELAXATION

One of the important skills which you can learn in relation to many areas of your life and performance is how to relax efficiently. Relaxation is probably one of the most important revision and life skills you can learn. Why?

- It helps you to control your performance.
- When you are relaxed you are more likely to use the energy you have, more effectively.
- It is the solid base upon which other mental coping strategies work. Such as positive self-talk, concentration and imagery.

THERE IS RARELY A GOOD PERFORMANCE WITHOUT RELAXATION.

Relaxation itself will not guarantee a good performance, but once you've learnt the skill and put it into use in a performance will you feel the benefit. If you are relaxed you're less likely to be stressed – you therefore give yourself a better chance to perform well.

Types of relaxation

There are many types of relaxation and any number of approaches are open to you. If you feel that you already have an efficient method of relaxation which you have found works, then keep it and work at it. It doesn't really matter which type of relaxation you use. You should adopt a technique which suits YOU and practice it regularly.

Most if not all the techniques rely on breathing as the common factor. You will find your revision easier and you will retain more information if you alternate periods of learning with periods of relaxation.

'... YOU CANNOT EXPERIENCE ANXIETY UNLESS YOU ARE BREATHING AS IF YOU ARE ANXIOUS.'
(MCLUGGAGE, 1977)

Relaxation techniques

When learning these relaxation techniques you should be in a comfortable position and in a quiet, warm environment. Once you have learnt them, try to use them in any environment under any conditions. Any one of these exercises will help – choose the one which you feel is most comfortable.

The quietest time of the breath is between exhaling and inhaling. Try to feel the stillness at that moment. When you can feel this quietness, you are learning how to relax. Try to concentrate on the body as you exhale fully and feel the tension leaving the body. Whenever you feel yourself getting too tense, try to feel the quiet time of the breath. You will feel a moment of peace and quiet by practising this exercise.

Rhythmic breathing

Inhale to a count of 4, hold for a count of 4, exhale to a count of 4, pause for a count of 4 before repeating the sequence. You may alter the rhythm of your breathing by changing the count.

Ratio breathing 1:2

Take a deep breath, and then exhale fully. Breathe again, to a count of 3 on the inhale, and a count of 6 on the exhale. If you run out of breath before reaching 6 then take a deeper breath and exhale more slowly. Try to be fully aware of the complete inhale and exhale cycle. Focus on how the body feels on the exhalation. When you become more practised you can deepen the relaxation by changing the count to 5:10 or 6:12 etc. This is a very effective relaxation exercise when you have learnt to do it properly. The exhale is the important part of this skill. Remember how good you feel!

Concentration breathing

Concentrate on focussing your attention on your breathing rhythm. If your mind wanders to something else during the breathing cycle, redirect your attention back to your next breath. Allow the intruding thought to disappear. Think of becoming more relaxed on each exhalation. This is a very good exercise to practise if you find yourself becoming distracted for whatever reason.

See yourself as being relaxed (Imagery)

Sit in a chair and develop a picture of yourself being very relaxed. You may see yourself lying on a beach in the sun, sitting in your favourite chair in your favourite room, or in a very tranquil place of your own choice. This can be a secret place unknown to anyone else. You develop it and keep it for yourself. Always SEE and FEEL yourself as being relaxed.

YOU: THE STUDENT

GOETHE
'WHATEVER YOU CAN DO, OR DREAM YOU CAN BEGIN IT. BOLDNESS HAS GENIUS, POWER AND MAGIC IN IT.'

The process of self assessment now takes a deeper look at you – the Student. Be aware that some aspects of what you have learned about your Self Concept will dictate how you behave as a student. This self knowledge will help you prepare and plan a suitable programme for yourself. You are not like anyone else; consequently your programme should be tailored to suit you.

How well do you know yourself as a student?
- Do you know – your best methods of learning?
- Do you know – how well you study?

IF YOUR PERFORMANCE IS IMPORTANT SO TOO IS YOUR PREPARATION

Exam preparation will not take over your life completely during the coming weeks, but it will certainly increase in importance. If something is important you have to take it seriously. Being serious means that you are concerned with being better, being more efficient – perhaps working for the same length of time, but obtaining greater reward from the time spent.

HOW DO YOU LEARN AND STUDY?

You have 100 billion brain cells, but how you use them is very important when trying to learn anything.

You basically learn through your senses in three main ways.
visual (seeing)
auditory (hearing)
kinaesthetic (feeling, doing)

Most educational situations, stress the more formal method of learning. They talk, you listen. This method of learning concentrates on books and talking in the form of lessons and lectures. This may not be enough by itself and therefore you may need to add other ways to help you learn more efficienctly. This may not be the most efficient way for you to learn at all. You are in the habit of learning in this formal way because that is the major approach used in most schools and colleges. Research from Harvard University tells us that you have more then one kind of intelligence – in fact you have seven.

YOU WILL ALMOST CERTAINLY USE ONE OF THESE WAYS MORE THAN THE OTHERS. IT IS VERY IMPORTANT TO KNOW FROM THE BEGINNING WHICH METHOD OF LEARNING YOU PRESENTLY USE.

1. **Your linguistic intelligence.** This means that you have the ability to talk and write well.
2. **Your mathematical intelligence.** This means that you are good with numbers and can think logically.
3. **Your visual intelligence.** This means that you have the ability to see in your mind's eye and to imagine how things might look. In other words you can visualise how things look.
4. **Musical intelligence.** This is the ability to create and interpret music. You can keep a rhythm. It is much easier to learn when you have a rhyme or music. You don't ever sit down and try to learn the words of 'pop' songs, you remember them because of the rhyme and the music.

5. **Physical intelligence.** This means that you have the ability to move well, build and construct things.
6. **Inter-personal intelligence.** This means that you have the ability to communicate well with others. You make other people feel good.
7. **Intra-personal intelligence.** This means that you have the ability to be self-analytical, objective and very quiet. You tend to understand yourself well. You create your own goals and plans to help you to succeed.

It is quite true that most 'academic' subjects are taught through only two of these 'intelligences', linguistic and the mathematical/logical intelligences. However, the main aim of this book is to help you to become very positive and confident about your learning and revising methods. This means that you have to first of all become aware of the main way you learn. (filling in the questionnaires will help you to do this.) You will probably use one or two of the senses more than the others, following this, organise and approach your work, decide which suits you best.

How do you learn? Let's find out!

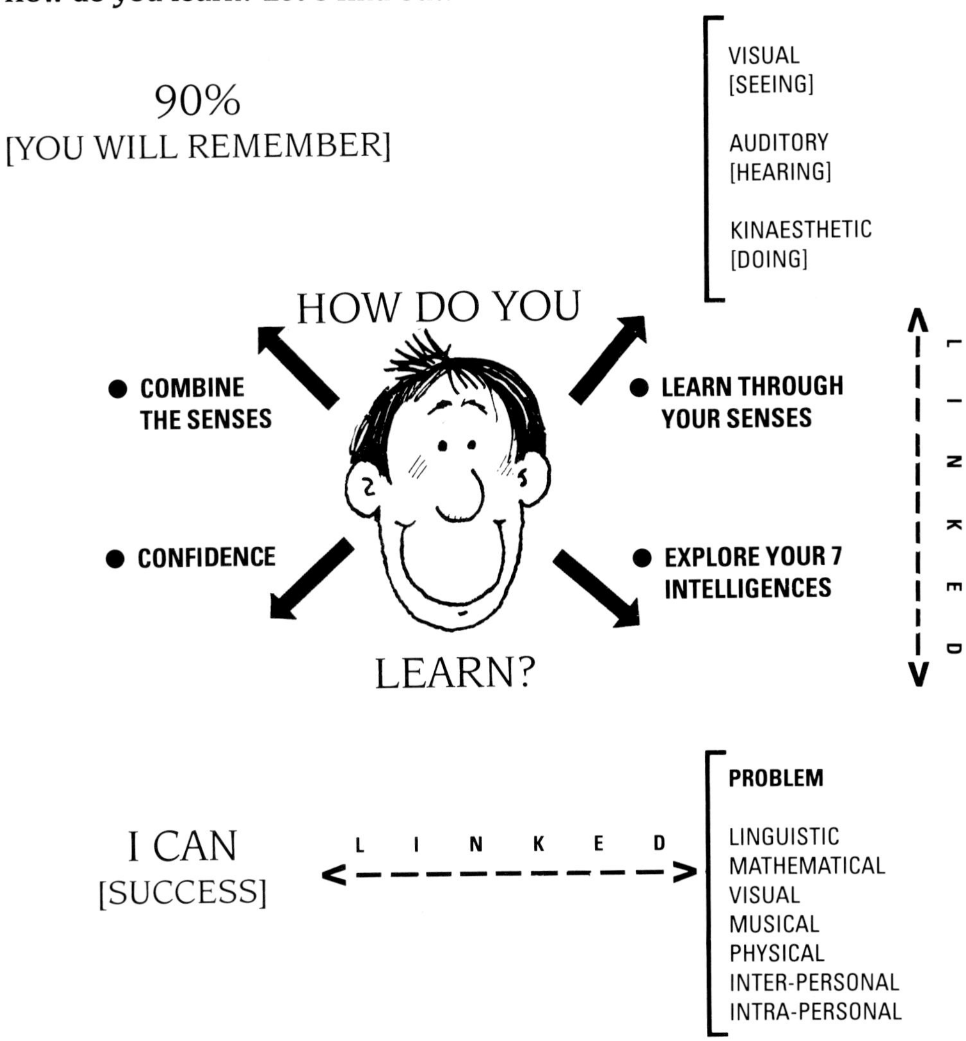

QUESTIONNAIRE 1:

HOW GOOD A STUDENT ARE YOU, WHAT DO YOU NEED TO WORK ON?

Fill in this questionnaire and try to be honest with yourself. It is personal to you and no one else is going to see the answers.

Each question is rated on a scale from 1 - 5.

1 – Not like me.
2
3 – Average
4
5 – Very much like me.

If when you have completed this questionnaire and have circled any 1's and 2's or 3's you may need more help with your revision programme and studying.

COMPLETE
MY LEARNING STRENGTHS ARE:

I NEED MORE HELP WITH

I am confident of my ability to learn things.	1	2	3	4	5
I know that there are different ways of learning.	1	2	3	4	5
I always set goals for my studying life/private life.	1	2	3	4	5
I have plans to make my goal work.	1	2	3	4	5
I make lists outlining the things I have to do.	1	2	3	4	5
I understand that I can control my own development.	1	2	3	4	5
I find studying easy.	1	2	3	4	5
I am not easily distracted.	1	2	3	4	5
I tackle new subjects in an organised way.	1	2	3	4	5
I take notes when reading or listening to a lecture	1	2	3	4	5
I often stop to think about the work I'm doing.	1	2	3	4	5
Text books don't worry me.	1	2	3	4	5
I like to get a general idea about a book before I look at it in detail	1	2	3	4	5
I'm good at asking myself questions as I am working and studying.	1	2	3	4	5
I sometimes use my own words to describe what I'm studying.	1	2	3	4	5
I write the key points of what I'm learning.	1	2	3	4	5
I write key words and points on cards.	1	2	3	4	5
I draw pictures and diagrams to illustrate what I'm learning.	1	2	3	4	5
I like to chat with friends about what I'm learning.	1	2	3	4	5
I keep reading my notes to remind myself of the important points.	1	2	3	4	5
I have a good memory for facts and figures.	1	2	3	4	5
I have no problem asking other people for help.	1	2	3	4	5
I am good at reviewing how I have learnt something.	1	2	3	4	5

QUESTIONNAIRE 2:

WHAT ARE YOUR BEST METHODS OF LEARNING?

Tick the response which best suits you.

1. Do you usually remember more from a class lesson when:
   a. You do not take notes, but listen very carefully.
   b. You sit near the front of the room and watch the teacher.
   c. You take notes (whether you use them again or not.)

2. Do you usually solve problems by:
   a. Talking to yourself or a friend.
   b. Using an organized, systematic approach like lists etc.
   c. Walking, pacing or some other physical activity.

3. Do you remember phone numbers (when you can't write them down) by:
   a. Repeating the numbers orally.
   b. 'Seeing' or visualizing' the numbers in your mind.
   c. 'Writing' the numbers with your finger on the table or wall.

4. Do you find it easier to learn something new by:
   a. Listening to someone explain how to do it.
   b. Watching a demonstration of how to do it.
   c. Trying it yourself.

5. Do you remember most clearly from a movie:
   a. What the characters said, background noises and music.
   b. The setting, scenery and costumes.
   c. The feelings you experienced during the movie

6. When you go to the supermarket do you:
   a. Silently or orally repeat the grocery list.
   b. Walk up and down the aisles to see what you need.
   c. Usually remember what you need from the list you left at home.

7. When you try to remember something do you:
   a. Try to see it happen in your mind.
   b. Hear in your mind what was said or the noises that occurred.
   c. Feel the way 'it' reacted with your emotions.

8. Do you learn a foreign language best by:
   a. Listening to records or tapes.
   b. Writing and using a workbook.
   c. Attending a class in which you read and write.

9. If you don't know how to spell a word do you:
   a. Sound it out.
   b. Try to see it work in your mind.
   c. Write the word in several different ways and choose the one that looks right.

10. Do you enjoy reading most when you can read:
    a. Dialogue between characters.
    b. Descriptive passages that allow you to create mental pictures.
    c. Stories with a lot of action in the beginning (because you find it difficult to concentrate early on).

11. Do you remember people you have met by their:
    a. Names.
    b. Faces.
    c. Mannerisms, movements etc.

12. Are you distracted mainly by:
    a. Noises.
    b. People.
    c. Environment (temperature, comfort of furniture etc.)

13. Do you usually dress:
    a. Fairly well (though clothes are not very important to you).
    b. Neatly (in a particular style).
    c. Comfortably (so you can move easily).

14. Do you have problems being active and sitting to read so you:
    a. Talk with a friend.
    b. Watch TV or look out of the window.
    c. Fidget in your chair, or can't lie still in bed.

Count the total number which fall into the following categories.

a ________ auditory (by hearing)

b ________ visual (by seeing)

MY BEST METHODS OF LEARNING ARE

c ________ Kinaesthetic (by touching, doing or moving)

Is any one response much higher than the others?

Are the results what you expected them to be? Did you see yourself in this way?

By now you may have found out that you learn best through the visual and the physical senses. This doesn't mean that you will not learn to write very well, all it means, is that, you will create pictures in your mind, or see the subject clearly through imagery, or remember your notes and key points through drawing pictures, or diagrams. Neither is there anything to prevent you from walking about whilst you're learning the work, or even acting it out if you want to! You will certainly learn your work more efficiently and will have a greater recall of the information which also means that you will feel more confident about your knowledge.

It doesn't really matter how you learn as long as you use the methods which best suit you. A combination of the use of all the senses and intelligences is the best way to learn.

SAYING HEARING SEEING AND DOING

It appears that on average you remember,

20% of what you read
30% of what you hear
40% of what you see
50% of what you say
60% of what you do

BUT 90% of what you say, hear, see, and do you will remember.

So go on combining as many methods of learning as possible.

A LEARNING MAP

Let's have a look at what you have learnt so far. One efficient method of doing this is to do it through a learning map. A learning map or mind mapping, summarises all the information you need to know in a visual way. Through pictures you are able to see all the information in a logical presentation, and it's easy to remember. To make your own learning map follow this process step by step.

1. Start in the centre with the subject, it can be anything, a book, a poem, a mathematical problem, a subject in Biology such as the environment.

2. Branch out from the centre adding relavant information and key words or statements. You can go on adding thoughts and information as long as you go on learning. You can also indicate which pieces of information are linked or related in some way.

3. Use as much colour as you wish, draw pictures, diagrams or logos. Capital letters will help to emphasise and most of all don't try to put too much on one page. Use larger paper and pin it up in your room. That way, you will see it, speak it, act it and visualise it as often as possible. This means that you build up your memory without you even realising it! You will also be able to 'see' your learning map in your mind's eye even though you may not be sitting looking at it. Very helpful in an exam or test situation!

YOU MAY FIND ONE OF THE WHITE BOARDS WHICH YOU USE FELT PENS ON VERY USEFUL. IT IS EASILY CLEANED AND USEABLE TIME AFTER TIME.

Keep experimenting with your learning maps. The more you practise the more relevant and informative they become. You can also have all of your revision notes on one page which is illustrated.

YOUR PHYSICAL WELL-BEING DURING EXAM PERIODS

How you feel physically during your exam period will have either a positive or a negative effect upon you. If you feel tired, physically exhausted, and not alert it will have a detrimental effect on how you will function during the exam period. Your physical well-being should not be ignored at any time of your life, but it is more important during times of added stress such as exams. Fill in the following questionnaire. It will give you some information regarding how YOU feel and deal with your physical well-being during exam periods. Be honest with yourself and try to do something about this important area of you as a student.

INDIVIDUAL PHYSICAL NEEDS DURING EXAMS

Physical

1. Do you need to take part in any physical activities during the revision and exam period? YES / NO
2. How often would you take physical activity during this period? ____________
3. If you do not engage in physical activity, what other forms of relaxation do you need during the revision and exam period? ____________
4. Why do you feel that you need to take any form of relaxation during this period? ____________
5. Do you feel guilty about going out and enjoying yourself during the revision and exam period? YES / NO
6. If YES explain why. If NO give reasons

____

Eating habits

7. Do your eating habits change before/during this period. YES / NO
8. If YES explain how. If NO, explain what your normal diet is

____

9. Do you feel that you need special treatment, or a special diet during exams? YES / NO
10. If YES, please explain why.

____

Sleeping Habits

11. Do you find it difficult to sleep normally during the revision and exam period YES / NO
12. If YES, please explain why.

____

13. On average how many hours sleep do you need during this period? ______________________

14. Is this more/less than you would normally require. MORE/LESS

15. Is there any other information that you feel is important in relation to your physical needs during the revision and exam period?

Once you have completed this questionnaire try to fit your physical requirements into the revision/exam period. Don't feel guilty about it. As an individual you need to get it right if you want to perform well in your exams. Inform parents of any needs – they also want to help!

YOUR STUDYING ENVIRONMENT

Now that you have a better idea of how you learn, how you study, and what your physical needs are likely to be during the preparation and performance periods, consider your best study options.

Begin by filling in the following questionnaire to help you to think about it in an objective way.

Under what conditions do you study best?	
	silence, background music, low noise or noisy sounds
	bright, medium or low light
	sitting up straight at a desk or relaxing on the bed or floor
	in the early morning, afternoon, evening or late at night
	being still or moving around

Once you understand under what conditions you study best, you would be well advised to make sure that, as far as possible, your own study conditions match your answers above. Try to make your parents, flat or room mates understand this, they will want to help you plan for success as well.

A word of warning . . . The conditions in which you enjoy studying may not be the same as those in the exam room when you finally take the exam. Silence . . . good light . . . formal setting . . . sitting at a desk . . . timed period . . . no chance for physical exercise like walking or running . . .

If your own study habits DO NOT match those of the exam room, you would be well advised to simulate the exam conditions when you get closer to the actual exam time. If you don't, they may cause you some anxiety. PRACTISE IT BEFOREHAND . . . Don't let the exam conditions be a cause of your stress, you'll have enough to think about without adding to your anxiety.

THE IMPORTANCE OF TIME CONTROL

TIME IS A CENTRAL CONCEPT TO EVERYTHING YOU DO, BECAUSE WHATEVER IT IS YOU DO, YOU DO WITHIN TIME. THEREFORE HOW YOU SEE AND HANDLE TIME IS AN IMPORTANT SKILL.

An important aspect of planning any performance, in this case your exam revision programme and the exam itself, is how you manage the time you have available to you.

Is your life disorganised and chaotic? Do you never have enough time to do the things you want to do? Do you feel frustrated and harried most of the time, so that small trivial matters use up much of your energy?

How often do you say to yourself,
"I would really have liked to do more revision but I never seemed to have the time". Where does the time go?

ONE BITE AT A TIME

The secret if you never seem to have enough time, is to learn how to be a "SMARTER" worker, not a "HARDER" worker. Being smarter means being a better ORGANISED worker. Try to follow these easy steps – don't panic, do one thing at a time

HOW TO CONTROL TIME

IMPROVING YOUR CONTROL OF TIME INVOLVES:

PLANNING =
Listing all the things you have to do in a given time period

SCHEDULING =
Measuring how long activities take before organising them within subdivisions of time.

MANAGING =
Sticking to the plan, adjusting it to meet the overall goal by adopting techniques personal to you.

START BY REVIEWING YOUR TIME CONTROL NOW

Begin as soon as you can to keep track of how you DIVIDE and USE your time. There are many ways to do this – you can probably devise a better one yourself – but the following is one example

Design a personal calendar for the whole period under review – try it at first for one week: For example:

MONDAY	TUESDAY	WEDNESDAY	THURSDAY	FRIDAY	SATURDAY	SUNDAY
AM						
PM						
EVE						

Then design a daily time log, the day being subdivided into sections which suit you:

TIME		ACTIVITY
MORNING	___ ___ ___	
AFTERNOON	___ ___ ___	
EVENING	___ ___ ___ ___	

Carry a daily time log with you until you have developed 'a planned time log', and on a daily basis, review how you spent your time. How much is 'work related', how much 'fun related' and how much 'nothing is happening time'?

This acts as a simple description of how you spend your time. Reviewing this log will help you to see whether any patterns emerge – how you use the time you have, how you waste the time you have, or whether you might find a little extra time. Once you have had some practise, you can begin controlling your time in earnest.

ONE OF THE KEYS TO GOOD TIME MANAGEMENT IS BEING ABLE TO PRIORITISE THE THINGS WHICH NEED URGENT ATTENTION.

STEP 1: **PLANNING**

LIST All the activities you know you have to do in a time period – work, family, social recreational, etc.

STEP 2: **SCHEDULE**

DRAW UP A daily/weekly time chart

DECIDE How you will use your time in relation to:

- Revision goals
- The stage of the programme you are at, eg. foundation, planning, familiarisation, learning or performance.
- Priority areas which need your attention.
- Personal goals.

ENTER Having estimated the durations of each activity, enter them onto the schedule using your order of priority.

There ought to be sometime every day when you give yourself permission to take time out and have fun. This can take the form of exercise, listening to music, TV, reading a novel, talking to friends etc. Your physical needs questionnaire will have given you some guidance.

STEP 3: **MANAGE**

YOU CAN ONLY DO SO MUCH IN ONE DAY. PLAN WISELY AND DO NOT FEEL GUILTY ABOUT WHAT YOU HAVEN'T DONE. IF YOU HAVE PRIORITISED CAREFULLY THEN IT WILL ALL GET DONE IN TIME.

REVIEW Your time log daily to determine how you are doing.

Analyse if you are trying to do too much or trying to handle too many priorities at once.

TIME ROBBERS **RECOGNISE AND ELIMINATE**
Those things which though not necessarily undesirable, will if you fail to recognise and do nothing about them, eat into your time. Telephone calls, unexpected visitors, parental demands (shopping, visiting, tidying rooms, girl/boyfriends except by arrangement.

DON'T WASTE TIME FEELING GUILTY ABOUT WHAT YOU HAVEN'T DONE. NOTHING AWFUL IS GOING TO HAPPEN TO YOU.
RELAXATION IS A PRIORITY – PROTECT IT!

STOP WORRYING AND START PLANNING.

Use the following groupings to help you categorise your work in order of priority.

SUBJECT ______________________

MUST DO NOW	MUST DO	DESIRABLE TO DO	CAN DO

THE IMPORTANCE OF MEMORY

All students know that memory is an important part of exam performances. They often worry about whether their memory will cope, but like any mental skill, it can be enhanced. Human beings do not actually forget information. The human mind remembers almost everything that happens to the person. The problem is that sometimes information cannot be recalled. What we actually mean when we say "I cannot remember" is that our memory is (temporarily) blocked.

Memory skills can be enhanced quite easily, by linking them to the learning methods that suits you best and knowing how best to deal with memory blocks.

THE MEMORY SYSTEM
The memory system shares brain cells and connections with each of your three brains – the primitive brain, which controls your breathing, your heart beat and primitive instincts such as your sense of territory; the middle brain, which controls your hormones, your health, your sexuality and your emotions; and the thinking brain which controls your thoughts.

The efficiency of the system depends on two things:

- How well each of the three brains and the connections between them are used.
- How good your memorisation behaviour is in dealing with memory blocks.

There are four stages of memory:

1. **The perception stage,** when we receive information through the senses.
2. **The encoding stage,** when we begin to try to understand and, select, organise and store the information in our short term memory.
3. **The storage stage,** when we groove and understand the information, through learning, repetition, familiarisation and then store in our long term memory.
4. **The retrieval stage,** when we recall the meaningful information which we have stored in long term memory.

STRATEGIES TO IMPROVE YOUR MEMORY

(Note, these strategies refer to the next three stages within this preparation).

STAGE 2: ORGANISATION
IN THE PERCEPTIONS STAGE information is received through any one of five senses. It is stored in four separate memories – verbal, visual, motor skill (or muscle) and factual.

Receiving information so that it can be easily stored requires the person to be:

- RELAXED, to make reception of information easier
- INTENT ON REMEMBERING to deliberately signal the system
- FOCUSED ON THE INFORMATION ignoring all distractions

IN THE ENCODING STATE information is welcomed to the memory system.

So that is can be stored for future recall the receiver must:

- BE SELECTIVE – not everything needs to be remembered
- ORGANISE INFORMATION into logical patterns, groups, links and associations
- FEED INFORMATION IN DIGESTIBLE QUANTITIES
- PLAN LEARNING PERIODS OF SUITABLE LENGTH

STAGE 3: FAMILIARISATION

IN THE STORAGE STAGE information is transferred from short to long term memory. For this to be successful information has to be deliberately processed, so that it is 'grooved' strongly into memory paths.

- FAMILIARISE YOURSELF OFTEN – to groove thought paths.
- MULTISENSORY FAMILIARISATION allows all your separate memories – sight, sound, feelings – to reinforce grooving
- REHEARSE the meaning of the information regularly
- ASSOCIATE the information with other information to increase meaning and reinforce grooving.
- SLEEP IS AN IMPORTANT PART OF MEMORY STRATEGY

STAGE 4: LEARNING

IN THE RETRIEVAL STAGE provided that information has been encoded correctly, and stored with due care and attention, there is no reason why recall should not be relatively easy.

THERE IS NOTHING WRONG WITH YOUR MEMORY

If you think calmly, you will realise that you can remember all kinds of things – songs, pictures, smells, dates, telephone numbers, names, experiences, feelings – all with very little difficulty. Try to recall occasions when:

- Information 'long forgotten' floats into your mind.
- A smell, a sound, an association conjures up a memory.
- Asked to do something you haven't done for years – swim or ride a bicycle – you do it without any problem.

CONCENTRATION AND DEALING WITH DISTRACTIONS

Concentration is the control of your attention. The ability to concentrate and deal with any distraction that causes you a problem, is said by some, to be the most important performance skill of all. If you can remain focused on what you have to do at any one moment, then you are controlling the right conditions for an effective and enhanced performance. Whenever your concentration deserts you, there is a lowering of performance.

The key to concentration is maintaining focus without being distracted by factors external to yourself – music, shouting, traffic noise, talk, or other people – or internal – feeling tired, nervous, day dream, thoughts of yesterday, or thoughts of tomorrow. Concentration is a mental skill which we all have, but because people are different, our abilities to concentrate in a particular way are different. Whatever you may think, your concentration is not all bad. We can all concentrate in some way, the secret is finding which way. The focus of concentration can be either broad – when you take in a lot of things at once – or narrow when you focus very precisely on one specific thing. This range of concentration can be either external, focusing on things outside yourself, or internal, the latter can include thoughts from the past, the present and the future.

For example:

I am feeling ill	broad internal
My big toe hurts	narrow internal
This room is cold and there are too many people	broad external
The hands of the clock are moving very fast	narrow external

Which type of concentration are you good at?

Are you better at:

- **Taking in a lot of information quickly** whilst unable to concentrate on one thing only for any length of time. Or Vice Versa.
- **Much better at planning and solving** the answer to the question without being able to focus on the anxiety messages from within you and controlling them.

You may find you are already quite skilful at two of the above, continue to work at them because they are your strengths. You will also have to give your attention to your weak areas of concentration, and this will give you the feeling of confidence you will need in all areas of concentration. In other words whatever happens in the exam situation, you will be able to cope with it.

'AS IN BUILDING UP PHYSICAL ENDURANCE, EFFECTIVE CONCENTRATION IMPLIES BUILDING UP MENTAL ENDURANCE.'
KUBISTANT. 1981

Another key feature of concentration is that it is a dynamic process. That is, in any one performance you continuously switch from one kind of focus to another, from broad to narrow, from internal to external. Once you have learned to focus more efficiently the next step is learning to sustain and pace it.

Begin this process by:
- Expanding the time you focus on an article/object.
- Try to expand the time each day that you focus on one object.

(You will learn just how long you can focus effectively before needing a break. Once you know this you can then begin to pace yourself). Only by learning what your 'optimal' time of attention is will you learn how to ease off. **Trying harder IS NOT the answer it only helps to destory and decrease your 'mental endurance' which you are trying hard to increase.**

How do you learn to concentrate?
Try some of these exercises to help you develop the skills.
You will need a quiet place to do any of the following exercises.

Exercise 1
This exercise helps you to become aware of your ability to focus on one thing only and then switching to a more open and general focus.

- Focus on a light in the room and take up a comfortable position and relax.
- Once you are relaxed, try to spend about one (1) minute focussing on the light. Try to feel all your mental energies focussing only on the light.
- Now become aware of the rest of the room within your field of vision. Take in as much detail of the whole room as possible, without moving your head.
- Now focus back in on the light. Then switch your awareness once again back to the whole room.

You can 'play' with this kind of exercise wherever you are for example:
Walking home – focus on one object close to you, than switch to become aware of everything around you.

Sitting in any room – focus on one object in the room, then switch to looking out of the window.

Remember to learn to recognise the feelings and sensations associated with one object or the general field. After ONE WEEK of exercising the switch of focus you will be able to apply this skill to any of your revision sessions, the practice of exam answers etc. You should try to switch focus from internal feelings, breathing, emotions to something external to you.

DO NOT feel guilty about taking time-outs, or relaxing from the prolonged periods of revision, writing or planning answers to questions. If you are going to be concentrating for 3 hours, the maximum time of exams, you have to establish how you will PACE yourself.

Relaxing before and during the exam is important because it helps to maintain good concentration.
The small 'time-outs', or relaxation breaks can vary:

a) making a cup of tea or coffee

b) shrugging shoulders

c) gazing out of the window

d) stretching different parts of the body

Everyone has a limit to the length of time they can focus. It is quite normal, and indeed important, to take short breaks.This also helps you to recall the information which you are trying to remember/learn. Most people find it difficult to really concentrate for more than 25 minutes. – Don't force yourself into long sessions – take TIME-OUTS. (Also check the section on Memory).

Naturally, as you learn to become more focused then you become less distracted. Your mind will not go off on all kinds of tangents and neither will it blank out. You are now in control of your performance and you are disciplining your mind. If the mind is not disciplined you will be open to distractions of all kinds. By focusing on the thing you need to do well is very good mental discipline and the goals you want to achieve will also help you to remain focused.

Exercise 2

This exercise will help you to increase your skill of focusing on a task whilst concentrating, scanning and storing information.

Scan the grid and within one (1) minute find and circle as many numbers as possible in numerical order beginning with 00.

You can increase the difficulty by:

a) selecting odd numbers ie. 00, 01, 03 etc.
b) selecting even numbers ie. 00, 02, 04, 06, etc.
c) find and circle numbers in descending numbers eg. 99, 98, 97, 96 etc.
d) do any of these exercises in a very distracting atmosphere – see if you can block out everything else and concentrate on the task in hand.

84	27	51	78	59	52	13	85	61	55
28	60	92	04	97	90	31	57	29	33
32	96	65	39	80	77	49	86	18	70
76	87	71	95	98	81	01	46	88	00
48	82	89	47	35	17	10	42	62	34
44	67	93	11	07	43	72	94	69	56
53	79	05	22	54	74	58	14	91	02
06	68	99	75	26	15	41	66	20	40
50	09	64	08	38	30	36	45	83	24
03	73	21	23	16	37	25	19	12	63

Grid exercise (Harris & Hart) 1984.

Dealing with distractions

One of the major causes of lack of concentration are distractions. Distractions fall into different categories.

Distractions in:

1. **The place** where you are working or performing (this could be, the school library, classroom, bedroom, the exam room itself, etc. – external to yourself).
2. **Your own body, thoughts and feelings,** (this could be feelings of anxiety, stress, tiredness, fear, tension etc. – internal to yourself).
3. **Relation to the other people involved,** (this could be teachers, parents, boy/girlfriends, friends, sisters/brothers, the examiner etc.)

In order to cope with any distraction, you first need to know what it is that distracts you.

THE METHODS BELOW ARE SKILLS WHICH YOU SHOULD PRACTICE AND USE WHEN NEEDED.

1. **The first exercise** for you to do is to make a list of the things in EACH CATEGORY which are your major distractions. Be honest and open with yourself. (place; feelings; other people).
2. **The next exercise, is to prioritise the distractions** which are the worst for you. In other words, they give you the biggest problems. Try not to worry about the ones left on the list, you may find that once you have dealt with the major distractions, the others seem to disappear!

Below are a few ways of dealing with each category of distraction.

Dealing with environmental distractions (the place)

1. Try to build the distraction into your mental imagery or any simulation of the exam conditions before the exam takes place. eg. if the distraction concerns noise, when trying to write under exam conditions, do it with noise in the background. On the other hand, if the distraction is silence, then you must practice writing in silent conditions.
2. Arrive early at the exam site and get used to the atmosphere, the temperature, the light, particular chairs etc.

What you are actually doing is 'making friends' with the distraction so that it will not bother you during your exam performance.

Dealing with body, thoughts and feelings distractions.

1. Take your performance cards with you, and very slowly and very thoroughly go through the details of last minute reminders. Try to really concentrate hard on the words and the meaning (refer to pages 44/138).
2. Alternatively, if the exam you are about to sit is based on essay writing, remind yourself of the techniques of essay writing. Once again, do it thoroughly and slowly.
3. Go through your own pep-talk with yourself and do some relaxation exercises at the same time. (Check pep-talk under anxiety).

All distractions in this category are from within you (internal), consequently most of the ways of dealing with them make you concentrate on things outside yourself. This shifts the concentration from worrying thoughts and feelings to other things like your notes, or your pep-talk. etc.

Dealing with the distraction of other people
One important fact about dealing with this category of distraction is that other people may drain you of confidence, and any belief you have in the things you are good at. You do not have to listen, switch off by using some of the skills below, or absent yourself from their company, or talk to them and explain how you feel, so that they will understand why you are behaving like this at this time.

Try some of the following skills.

1. Try to acknowledge their presence, and tell yourself. 'I know you are there, but you will not bother me, because you are not a threat to me.' This means you make friends with the distraction, acknowledge it, and get on with what is important to you.
2. Use the quiet place technique outlined below. This is a very good technique, which can be used for many things, including dealing with distractions (This is also very good for dealing with STRESS).
3. If all else fails, try to pay a lot of attention to your exam equipment which you have with you, eg. your pen, ruler, ink, cartridges, roll of sweets, pencils, pencil sharpener, calculator etc. This really means concentrating on them so that your focus of attention switches from other people to your equipment. This in itself will bring down your feelings of stress attached to the distraction.

THE QUIET PLACE

Imagine yourself alone and undisturbed in your favourite quiet place. It can be anywhere you wish, by the sea, in the mountains, or any place where you feel quiet, relaxed and peaceful. Use your imagination.

Become very aware of your favourite place and see yourself in it. See as much detail of colour, sound, touch, feel etc, as you can.

Recognise the real feeling of quietness and peace. Really immerse yourself in the feel of this quiet place.

With your eyes open bring your attention back to the room you are sitting in and very gently clench your fist. As you do allow yourself to go back to your quiet place and immerse yourself in it once more. Notice all the details of the quiet place once again. Feel really relaxed and at peace. Repeat this process of allowing the scene to fade and then clench your fist before returning to the quiet place. Do this 2 or 3 times before releasing your fist and opening your eyes.

WHAT EXPECTATIONS DO YOU HAVE?

As a student you will of course, have some idea about what you expect from yourself in relation to the exams. You may feel very confident about some subjects but not confident about others. Expectations – yours and other people's – are a major factor which will affect your performance. Expectations can be a positive guide for you or they can be destructive and a problem for you.

It is mainly the expectations of others which normally cause you the biggest problems. You may feel pressure from parents, teachers, your group of peers or even a nationally recognised pressure. Apart from this you also put pressure on yourself by your own expectations.

Expectations are linked with goal setting which has already been dealt with. However, it is important that you set yourself some expectations which will guide your planning and preparation.

These are naturally built around the information you get from others and that which you believe yourself. The skill is setting the expectations at the appropriate level. If you set them too high then you will not be motivated to try to achieve them, but if you set them too low you will also become demotivated because you find them too easy. The procedure is exactly like setting yourself goals about other areas of your life, only this time you are setting them in relation to the subjects you are taking in the exam.

Follow the next exercise and complete it very thoroughly. At the end you will have a much better idea of what you can expect in each of your subjects. It also gives you a framework which will help you to plan the areas of work which you have prioritised as needing more work, whilst at the same time giving you the confidence in other areas which you feel you know well.

Keep in mind the old Chinese proverb:

'EVERY JOURNEY OF A THOUSAND MILES STARTS WITH A SINGLE STEP.'

Estimating your expectations in your exam subjects also begins with a step at a time. Don't panic. Keep calm and be very objective about the answers you give in relation to each of the subjects you are working at.

LEARNING TO USE YOUR STRENGTHS

In each of the following examples the student was asked:

'On a scale of 0 - 10, (0 being awful and 10 being as good as you feel your preparation in each subject is AT THE MOMENT), where would you place yourself?'

THE EXAM PERFORMANCE IS YOURS. IT DOESN'T BELONG TO ANYONE ELSE. TAKE OWNERSHIP OF IT AND BE CONFIDENT ABOUT YOUR OWN EXPECTATIONS IN EACH OF YOUR SUBJECTS.

Student No. 1

0 ————●———————— 10

4

awful — as good as it can be at the moment.

This student has estimated that at the time of asking the preparation is at about 4. This performance has been estimated at about 40% good. In other words the student believes that he/she knows and understands well at least 40% of the subject. Even if this student did no more work, and he continued to really believe in the 40% good, and he was lucky with the exam questions, then a pass may be the result. Not a very good one and a bit chancy but who knows. But if at any time there is worry about the 60% of work not known then this student would almost certainly not pass the exam! Real confidence in the 40% does give a chance.

Student No. 2

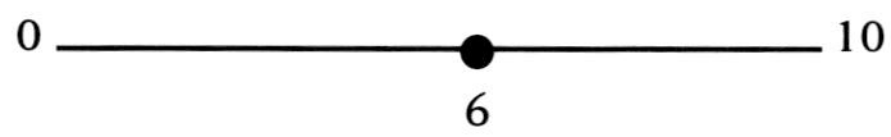

This student has estimated that at the time of asking, the preparation in the subject is at about 6. This performance has been estimated at about 60% good. In other words the student believes that 60% of the subject is well known, understood and learnt.
On this evidence, this student would easily pass the exam, if he/she really believes and has real confidence in the 60% knowledge they already have. However, if, at any time the student worries about the 40% not known then this will sabotage the 60% and lessen the chances of passing. If the student really panics about the 40% then a failure is likely to be the case.

Student No. 3

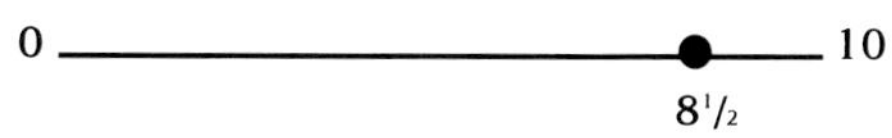

This student has estimated that at the time of asking, the preparation in the subject is at about $8\frac{1}{2}$. This performance has been estimated at about 85% good. No problem about passing the exam, especially if the student believes in the 85%, an excellent result would be the outcome. Even though 15% of the performance is not as good! However, if at any time this student panics about the lack of ability in the 15% then he/she lessens the chances of obtaining a really good pass.

Each student was then asked to write down what were the strengths, the good things which made up the 40%, 60% and 85% of the performance. They were then told to keep repeating what they could do from the lists they had written. I can do . . ., I do know my . . ., I feel confident about . . ., My . . . and my . . . are good, I am beginning to be well prepared. etc.

Each student then wrote a list of the things which still needed some work in the performance, and was asked to prioritise the items, i.e. which items need the least work for them to become strengths. An exercise like this reminds you of what you can do already, and what needs continued work. It also helps to keep reminding you of your strengths. It gives you something positive and good to say to yourself and about yourself.

What normally happens is that you become worried or even panicked about what you don't or can't do and forget what you can do.

ALWAYS REMEMBER WHAT YOU CAN DO.

Let's go back to our students.

Follow these simple steps to help you to plan your own expectations and recognise your strengths in each subject.

1. Estimate your own performance on the 0 - 10 scale regularly during your preparation.
2. Always list the strengths and the areas which need more work.
3. Keep talking positively to yourself about all the good things you know you can do.
4. Prioritise the 'needs more work' list. Work at the areas which need little work to make them into strengths.
5. Really believe and have confidence in your strengths and 'run with them'.
6. Don't be tempted to panic about the areas you don't know, but work at them, a little at a time. They will then become strengths and your estimated performance goes up. YOU CAN DO IT.

Use the form below to help you to deal with each of your subjects in a logical and honest manner

To gain maximum benefit, this exercise should be done approximately once every two weeks.

SUBJECT.	DATE.
STRENGTHS	**AREAS WHICH NEED MORE WORK**
ESTIMATED PERFORMANCE ON A 0____________________10 SCALE	

FEAR OF FAILURE

It is quite understandable, that at some time you may feel that you fear failing the exams. This may be normal in certain circumstances, but it should only be a fleeting thought before you dismiss it from your mind. If you plan properly, get the right level of expectation and feel confident, you should have no fear of failing.

If you continue to dwell on what you fear, then you will undoubtedly attract your fears. Focus on what you want. Dwelling on your fears will bring them upon you. Some of you will remember being so afraid of failing that you had sleepless nights or actually became sick before an exam or some other kind of performance.

YOUR MIND AND YOUR THOUGHTS ARE MAGNETS.

As pressures to succeed from parents, teachers, friends, and yourself increase, the possibility of failure may become more apparent. Most of the time these kinds of fears are linked with our self pictures. You equate failing with the knowledge that you are a failure as a person anyway! If you allow the fear of failure to take hold of you, you usually imagine all the worst possible things that could happen in the exam. Your mind will go blank, the right questions won't come up, you will be late arriving and they won't let you in, or you may become ill and won't be able to do the exam anyway.

Such fears set your mind on a negative cycle, and the more you think about it and imagine such things happening, the more you will actually ensure failure. The more your fears set your mind on a negative cycle, and the more you think about it and imagine such things happening the more you will actually ensure failure. The more your fears of failing enter your thinking the more the performance in the exam becomes badly affected. A poor performance will be the result.

Try not to feel trapped, that is, you may feel that you can't get out of the negative cycle and you don't know what to do. You can do this by putting together an effective programme for yourself. Such a programme should include most of the mental skills in this book plus the belief that you do know the subject and believe in your own ability, at whatever level.

YOU CAN GET OUT OF SUCH A CYCLE BY LEARNING TO CONTROL YOUR THINKING!

The important skills are:

- **A well established and effective goal setting programme.** Especially by beginning to focus on the performance rather than on the outcome. In this way you will allow yourself to have some small successes as you go along. (Check the motivation and goal setting sections in the book.)
- **A sound self-talk programme based on your strengths.** These strengths come from all areas of the performance. Your knowledge, your physical well-being, your mental skills, your technical skills of writing, planning, and strategising your answers, etc.
- **Facing up to the areas which** you think are areas which need more work. Plan to work at these as part of your goals and remember to do it slowly. ONE STEP AT A TIME – TAKE SMALL BITES. They will soon become strengths if you work at it in this way.
- **Making sure that you have a positive picture** of yourself being successful. See yourself writing very good answers, and try to know what it FEELS like to be successful. (Check the Imagery section).

Estimating your expectations in your exam subjects also begins with a step at a time. Don't panic. Keep calm and be very objective about the answers you give in relation to each of the subjects you are working at. Expectations derive from feelings and knowledge you have about yourself and information other people give you about yourself, eg. your teachers, friends and parents.

PLANNING THE ROUTE MAP OF YOUR PREPARATION

SUCCESSFUL PERFORMANCES ARE PLANNED AND PREPARED. Remember that in planning your programme you are also planning your OWN DEVELOPMENT and that development requires CHANGE.

PLANNING THE PERSON

1. YOU
   Come to terms with what kind of a person you are, but be aware that your Self Concept can be enhanced by self enhancement skills.

2. YOUR SELF CONFIDENCE
   Is your own personal barometer.

3. MOTIVATION IS VITAL FOR SUSTAINED WORK
   Your motivation strategies all depend on your understanding what is motivating you. Why you are/are not working?

4. ANXIETY WILL ALWAYS BE A PART OF PERFORMANCE
   Your anxiety will need some attention. First check what you are like naturally. Then, if you think you will need them practise RELAXATION skills as early as you can.

PLANNING: YOU THE STUDENT

1. LEARNING AND STUDYING
   There are two avenues of change and development. Understand the point at which you start and how you can improve.

2. PHYSICAL WELL-BEING
   Your physical needs will probably change during the exam performance period, if not before. You will need to give some attention to this. It is a good habit to get into anyway!

3. STUDY ENVIRONMENT
   This will affect the success of your programme if for no other reason than the amount of time involved. Take care also to compare your chosen conditions with those of the exam performances.

4. CONTROLLING TIME
   Use it wisely and efficiently and you will have plenty of time for everything, including free time. Don't feel guilty about this – everyone needs free time!

5. EXPECTATIONS
   What you expect of yourself in your exam subjects is an important exercise for you. Try not to fear failure. It won't happen – because you will plan too well.

6. CONCENTRATION
   Develop your powers of concentration and learn to control distractions.

You now have the knowledge to use when preparing a plan for your development and a plan for your success. Be methodical, thoughtful and honest with yourself. Base the plan on the answers you get, and you're ready for the next stage.

CHECK LIST		
AREA OF WORK	**DEALT WITH IT'S O.K.**	**NEEDS MORE ATTENTION**

PLANNING YOUR EXAM PERFORMANCE

WHAT DO YOU WANT TO ACHIEVE?

YOUR OUTCOME

August

BUT
You won't achieve this simply by saying " will!"

HOW WILL YOU ACHIEVE IT?

June

WHAT FEELING DO YUU WANT TO HAVE WHEN YOU ENTER THE EXAM ROOM?

(Students have said the same thing for years and years! You will probably say the same).

Late June

HOW WILL YOU ACHIEVE THIS FEELING

BY BEING IN

May

WHAT DO YOU NEED TO CONTROL?

Control is achieved by doing the right things. What are the right things?

Now

YOUR SELF	**YOUR STUDY**	**YOUR WORK**	**YOUR LIFE**
Concentration Motivation Self Talk	Time Place Priority Distractions	Knowledge Use of Knowledge	Interests Time Priority

A suggested answer to these routes map can be found in the Appendix.

PLANNING THE ROUTE MAP OF YOUR PREPARATION

Start with: Analysis of – Yourself / The Tasks

THE ROUTE MAP:

THE OVERALL PLAN OF CONTROL

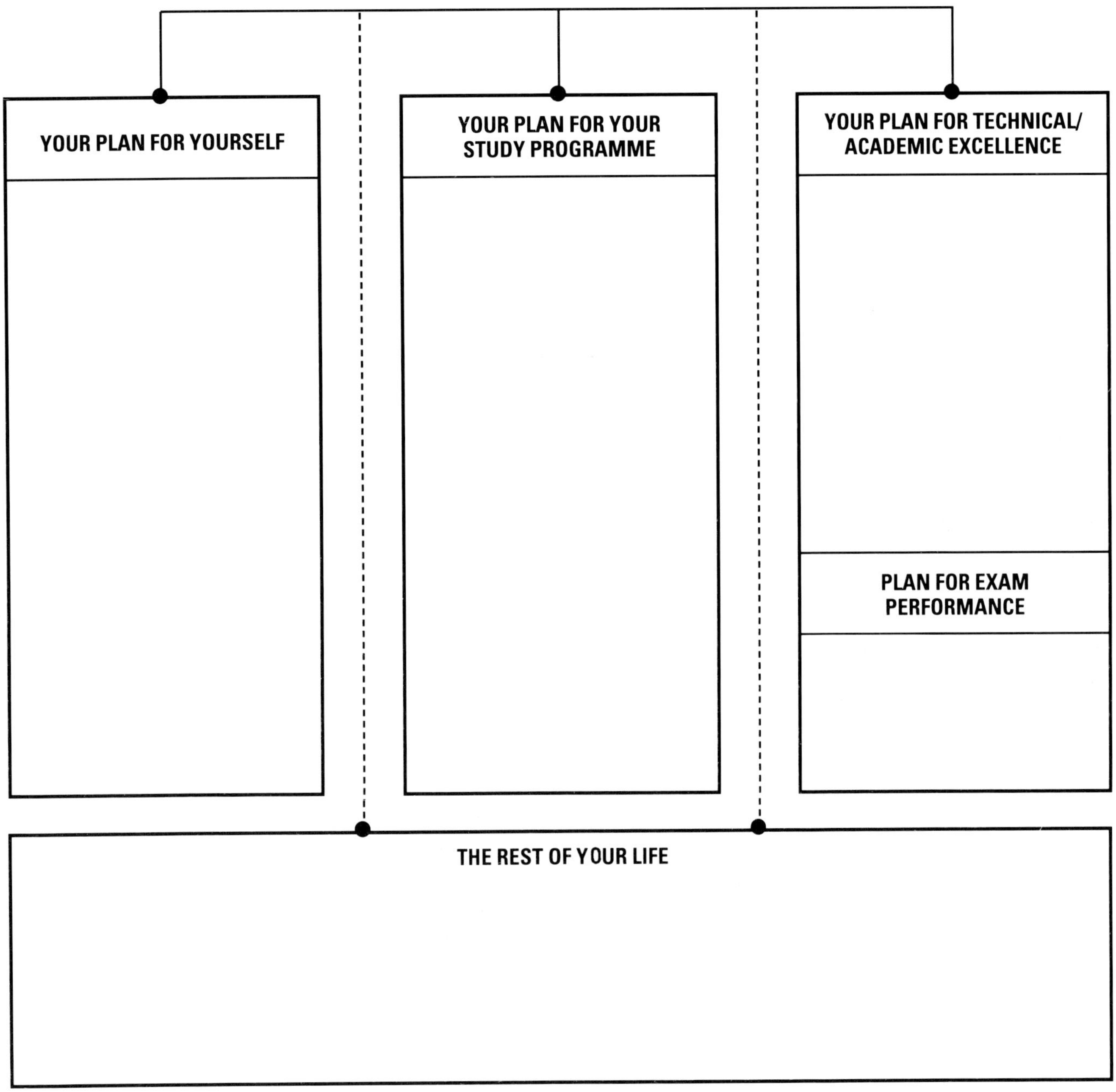

ABOVE ALL – DON'T PANIC
FOLLOW THE SIMPLE GUIDELINES FOR EACH SECTION
STAY IN THE PRESENT
'EVERY JOURNEY OF A THOUSAND MILES STARTS WITH A SINGLE STEP'

STAGE 2

ORGANISATION

INTRODUCTORY THEMES

The Organisation Stage changes the focus from internal to external, from the student to the work to be done. This allows the student to experience controlling a widening range of performance elements, but without the pressure of actual exam performances. The importance of this stage cannot be overstressed. It is a crucial part of every student's success style, the impact of which will be felt progressively through the remainder of the programme and in final performance. (If you are unsure of this refer to page 28)

THE TIMING OF THE ORGANISATION STAGE

Exactly when a student begins the Organisation Stage of the programme will depend on their lifestyle, responsibilities, commitments, and whether or not they are studying at a formal educational establishment. If they are, The Organisation Stage will probably coincide with a holiday period, allowing plenty of extra time to control the new work load. If they are not, the increasing demands of preparation will have to be met by either starting earlier, or reducing the range of activities within their lives.

PACE AND INTENSITY

The intensity of work should be high – at times you should certainly be working 'flat out'. Longish work periods of two, even occasionally three hours, can be used, for the work is chiefly physical and mechanical rather than mental.

GETTING STARTED

Getting started sounds very simple, but it may be more difficult than you think:

How easy is it for you to get started?

Do other activities in your life seem more attractive?	YES/NO
Do the tasks ahead of you seem too large?	YES/NO
Do the exams seem too far in the distance to worry?	YES/NO
Is that magazine more inviting than your study target?	YES/NO
Do you wonder what is on TV tonight?	YES/NO
Are you half waiting for the telephone to ring?	YES/NO
Do you keep putting off the work for 'just one more day'	YES/NO
Are you behaving like an ostrich – putting your head in the sand and hoping the work will away?	YES/NO

If it is a problem for you, take comfort: it is a problem many people experience. It is not at all exceptional. But, if you are going to accept the challenge – you have to start. Here are some suggestions which might help.

STRATEGY 1: ATTUNE TO THE IDEA
Think about the task for a day or two

Choose a day that will make the start easy (i.e. a day at the beginning of a week, free of any activity)

Make the decision to start deliberately and physically:

Make a formal contract with yourself

Enter the date in your diary

Make a formal preparation diary

STRATEGY 2: MAKE A FORMAL CONTRACT WITH OTHER PEOPLE
Your preparation will start on a specific day. Support this decision by:

Parents and/or teachers witnessing and signing the contract.

Parents agreeing to 'make sure' you do start when agreed.

Your own Self Talk: Talk positively and excitedly to yourself about your work. Tell yourself 'I can . . . I will'. If excuses prevail, become severe, Ask: Is studying really a priority? Is this just another excuse . . .!

STRATEGY 3: START WITH PHYSICAL ORGANISATION
Start with an activity related to study rather than study itself. Organise and layout your study area to your satisfaction. Collect, organise and label all files and notebooks.

Once a start has been made, make sure it is really good. Keep going, through two or three days extensive work without a change of focus to other activities. This will allow you to obtain a real 'feel' for the work. It will also do wonders for your confidence and your self esteem.

WHEN YOU DO START, MAKE IT GOOD!

ADOPT A PERFORMANCE ROUTINE: IT WILL HELP TO KEEP YOU GOING

A preparation routine, entered into every time you begin work, not only links work sessions together, but puts you into a professional 'study mode'.

FOR INSTANCE YOU MIGHT:
Always begin on the hour or half hour,
Always sit in your chair the same way, pushing your hips back against the backrest and deliberately sitting upright.
Always relax using a deep breathing technique,
Always pause to remind yourself of your goal, your plan, your determination to work,
Always do something physical – take off your watch, place it on the table in front of you, roll up your sleeves, etc.
Always use positive self talk

Having a personal work place is also a very good idea.

ORGANISING

YOUR STUDY PLACE

The place in which you study is very important. It will have a major influence on both the effectiveness of your work and the enjoyment you feel doing it.

Ernest Hemingway in 'Death in the Afternoon' says that when bulls run into the bullring they instinctively settle where they feel safe. Human beings are the same. We all have our preferred comfort zones in which we feel secure and 'at home' – shy students often sit in corners, unruly students at the back of a class, teachers sit on desk tops, while Headmasters often sit behind desks of gargantuan proportions.

Your chosen area should be:
Quiet, well lit, and well ventilated, away from any major distractions.

It should contain:
A desk or table of spacious dimensions
Space for books and files
Collection of pencils (different colours), pens, calculators and other equipment
A Display Board
An Upright Chair and a comfortable chair.

Your special study place – it might be a whole room, or only a part of a room – will contribute to the seriousness of your study habit, your attitude and your determination, and by your having all relevant books to hand, it will help you control time (when books are to hand they aren't a time robber).

MOST IMPORTANTLY YOUR STUDY AREA WILL BECOME A PART OF YOUR STUDY ROUTINE

YOUR LIFE

As your final performance comes a little closer, it is important to prioritise the different activities which are a part of your life. Although the range of activities might be beginning to narrow, your life is likely to be still very full – maybe fuller than you think!

To establish the range of activities in your life fill in the tables below:

SECTIONS OF YOUR LIFE	List of Major Activities involved
Family / Home	
Occupation / Work	
School / College / Univ.	
Social	
Personal	
Leisure	

PERFORMANCE PREPARATION	List the number of subjects and papers

WHAT ABOUT A HOLIDAY?

With Easter often occurring during the Organisation Stage, there might be a clash between your preparation and holidays. After looking at the list of activities in your life, additional to preparation, you might be forgiven for feeling that you need a holiday! Such a decision needs careful consideration. Holidays are personal. They can work for you or against you:

HOLIDAYS

Work for you by:	Work against you by:
Enabling you to relax	Increasing anxiety
Increasing freshness	Using up valuable time
Increasing commitment	Reducing commitment
Giving a change of focus	Being a distraction
Increasing control of work – when you restart	Making it more difficult to get started

Write down the factors which might:

Work for you	Work against you
______________________	______________________
______________________	______________________
______________________	______________________

GROUP TOURS

Group tours are holidays of course, but often they are holidays with a difference. Usually lasting a week or a few days longer and involving an invitation to join a national, representative school or college team, or a special group of friends, they engender unique feelings of excitement or enjoyment. Often they appear 'something not to be missed'.

Frequently schoolteachers and college tutors disapprove. They see them as 'irresponsible distractions'. Implicitly they believe that if a student is not involved in such activities they will be studying. This might be true, but equally it might not. In any case, such tours can be beneficial. They can increase a students' self esteem substantially as well as being exactly the kind of distraction to increase determination and narrow the focus.

Only once have I had personal experience of leading a school tour at April, but for the past fifteen years I have been involved with England Schools rugby players, very few of whom seemed to suffer adversely from the experience. For the most part such experience enhanced rather than diminished preparation.

HOW DO YOU FEEL ABOUT ALL THESE ACTIVITIES?

You may feel quite OK. In which case – fine! Or, you might feel a bit bewildered – similar to driving a car into a snowstorm at night, the headlights picking out the snowflakes driving at you like gunshot! If this second reaction is how you feel – relax, it need not remain like this. Provided that all activities are purposefully brought within your preparation strategy no harmful effects should occur.

YOUR TIME

Organising and managing your time requires you to use in a skilful way the techniques described in the Planning Stage (page 58). Design a calendar for the whole period to give you an overview. Schedule immediately all activities to which you have decided to remain committed – birthday parties, family weddings, a holiday, a group tour etc.

Schedule next, your programme a week at a time. The following schedule, which totals 37 hours of work time with quite a number of hours of unscheduled time, might be taken as a good indicator. If six hours per day are used for work, an average effective working week of 42 hours is possible. If the average is increased to eight hours a day, 56 hours per week is possible.

Use a schedule that divides the week into weekdays and weekends and each day into five study sections:

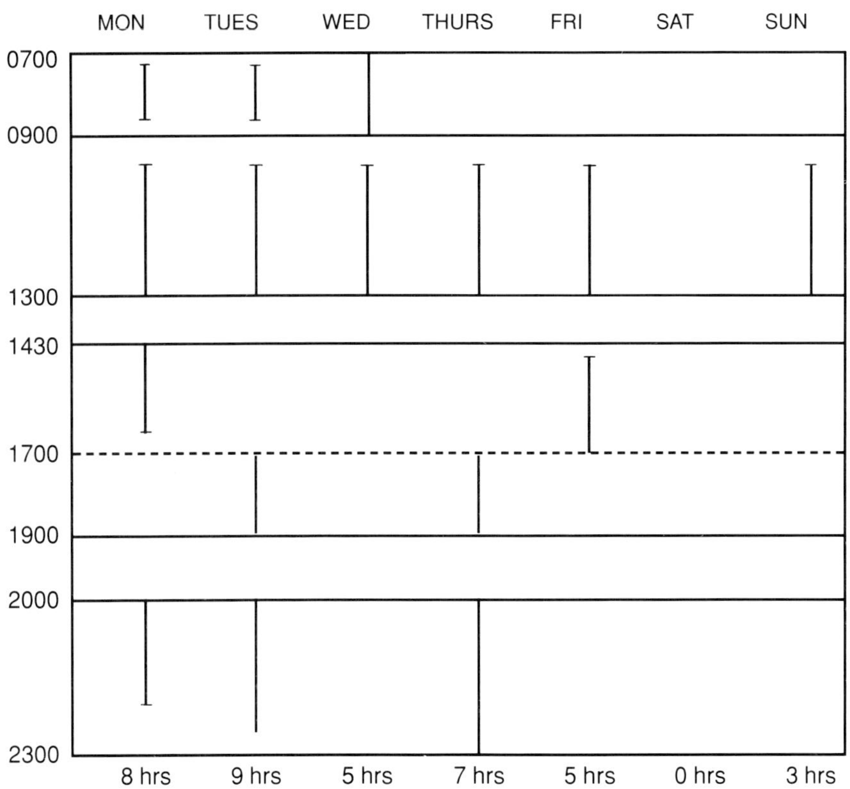

Finally, in order to maintain tight management control, schedule day by day using the kind of time log itemised on page 59 in the Planning Stage or see the Appendix where other examples are given.

THE FOLLOWING GUIDELINES WILL HELP YOU TO PLAN TIME EFFICIENTLY

Routine

Try to develop a routine. People generally like routines because they feel a sense of control.

Balance and variety
Every routine should have balance and variety. Some people like to vary day by day, others week by week. In arriving at your own balance be aware of different activities and work patterns.

Maintain momentum
Monday and Tuesday should be major work days to give you a feeling of progress.

Be flexible
Don't schedule every hour of every day; leave room for the unexpected and for change.

Freshness
Analyse your feelings to find out which periods of the day are best for you. Try to work when you are freshest, which with many people (but perhaps not you) is in the mornings.

Early Morning
If you haven't tried working before breakfast try it to see if it works for you. Your day will be off to a fast start which gives you a feeling of control – but don't try it after a late night.

IT'S YOUR TIME, YOU CONTROL IT AND PLAN IT. YOU CAN USE IT FOR MANY DIFFERENT THINGS EVEN ENJOYING YOURSELF.
GET THE BALANCE RIGHT AND YOU WILL SUCCEED.

Weekends
Leave weekends 'free' – for relaxation, leisure and for catching up.

YOUR WORK

Your work during the Organisation Stage is very specific.
1. Organising the syllabus for each of your exam subjects.
2. Writing your Performance Scripts in such a way as to facilitate understanding and recall

YOUR SYLLABUS
The syllabus (of each of your courses), the specific body of knowledge necessary for you to perform, is the examiner's starting point. It should also be yours.

Teachers and Course Directors will be able to provide printed copies of the syllabus being studied. If, for some reason, this is not the case, complete formal syllabi can be obtained from the relevant Examination Board, the addresses of which can be found in Appendix page 174.

ANALYSE THE SYLLABUS
Look first at:
The aims of the syllabus and objectives of the examination (printed at the beginning of every booklet).

These are the examiner's goals; they help you to understand why the syllabus has been written and what skills the examination sets out to test.

This is essential information for anyone aiming to demonstrate a high level of skill. Yet surprisingly few students bother to do this (some teachers don't bother either!). Don't allow this to happen!

Consider next, the type and style of the examination:
How many papers are involved? What is their duration? Is the style different – Data Response, Essay, Case Study. Is the format different – questions compulsory or voluntary? What range of choice? Are there different / discrete sections? Do mark allocations differ? Is the content different – which sections of the syllabus do they assess? What resources are provided – atlas, tables, etc?

Finally, consider the detail, 'the route map' of the syllabus:
Most syllabi are little different to a novel, the story being told in sequential stages. All will have a logical pattern to them, which provides a link from stage to stage.

Analysing the total syllabus, understanding why and how it has been put together, enables you to physically feel the size of the job in front of you, like weighting an apple in your hand or seeing all the pieces of a jigsaw completed.

NEXT PATTERN THE TOTAL SYLLABUS (of each of your subjects)
READ THROUGH THE FORMAL SYLLABUS
There is always more than one way to travel any journey. When reading the formal syllabus provided by the Examination Board, bear in mind that it may have been compiled with a different purpose to your own. Your teachers too may have taught the syllabus in a different order.

The way you decide to divide the syllabus will probably adhere to the order in which it was taught, but be aware that any pattern which appears logical to your understanding is acceptable at this stage of the game.

DIVIDE MAJOR TOPICS WITHIN EACH SEGMENT

Eg: English History / European History
Microeconomics / Macroeconomics
Social Geography / Physical Geography

DECIDE MAJOR TOPICS WITHIN EACH SEGMENT
These divisions should satisfy your needs and understanding of the syllabus rather than those of the Examiner.

GROUP SIMILAR CONCEPTS WITHIN TOPICS
Concepts which are similar, or related, are probably already grouped within the same topic. Sometimes however, it helps to move concepts around according to your own needs.

When organising the contents of the syllabus into a pattern to suit your needs, use two principles – Digestive Pieces, The Magic Five. Both are fully explained when writing the Performance Script on page 96.

An example of a pattern syllabus. The Business Studies 'A' Level Syllabus of the Cambridge Examination Board.

Financial Aspects

Final Accounts
Profit and Loss
Balance Sheet
Definitions
Principles and Conventions
Reports

Final Accounts Analysis
Ratios
Other Tools – Comparisons Trends
Writing Reports

Source of Funds
Depreciation
Capital Gearing
Types of Finance
Sources of Finance

Valuation of Assets
Valuation
FIFO, LIFO
Inflation and Accounts
Revaluation

Budgeting
Concept of Budgets
Purpose of Budgets
Cash Budget
Manufacturing
Std. Cost Budgets
Capital Budgets
Rate of Return
Payback
NPV, DCF

Quantitative Aspects

Statistical Techniques
Presentation Data
Questionnaires
Standard Deviation
Index Numbers
Averages / Moving Averages

Distribution/Forecasting
Normal
Binormal

Operational Research
Concepts
Network Analysis – CPA
Linear Programming – Transportation
Simulation
Queuing Theory

Work Measurement
Work Study
Work Measurement
Value Analysis

Probability/Decision Trees
Expected Value

Economic A

MACRO ECONOMICS

Economic System

Government Policy
Fiscal
Monetary
External
Direct Control

Economic Problems
Inflation
Unemployment
Balance of Payment

MICRO ECONOMICS

Marketing
Intro Concepts
Marketing Mix
Intro questions
Price, Product, Promotion, Place

Production Control
Types of firms
Stock Control
Value Analysis
Location of Industry
Production Systems

Costing Analysis
Overhead Allocation
Costs and Pricing Policy
Breakeven Analysis

Human Aspects

Organisation
Concepts/Theories
3 Basic schools of thought
Formal/Informal
Principles of organisation

People in Organisation
Groups – definitions
Behaviour of Groups
Hawthorne Experiments

Leadership
Definitions
Qualities
Styles
Theories
Examples

Motivation
Definition
Types of Motivation
Theories
Methods

Communication
Definition
Types
Problems
Methods

Behaviour in the workplace
Strikes
Types
TU in workplace
Personnel Management

NEXT, PRIORITISE THE SYLLABUS

In any performance situation very few people are able to say 'I have done everything.' There simply isn't enough time or energy. Therefore it is crucial to concentrate on what MUST be done. Prioritising the syllabus enables you to do this; to decide the chief focus of your work, your own personal route map – based on:
The areas of the syllabus which are most likely to be a part of your performance, your strengths and your weaknesses.

The emphasis that your teachers placed on each section of the syllabus, together with the time they allocated, should already be sufficient to determine the more important areas. By far the best way however, is to analyse in detail, past exam papers. These should be obtainable either from your teacher or from the Examination Board.

The last five years papers are all that are needed to see the range and frequency of typical performance questions. Provided that topic areas (which deal with a wider range of knowledge) rather than specific questions (which are too narrow) are used, such an analysis will allow you to predict, with reasonable certainty, the type of question you will face in your own final performance.

TECHNICAL PRIORITISING

Analysis requires:
A set of past papers, sheets of A4 size paper, an active mind 'to ask the right questions'

Organise your sheet of A4 paper:

TOPIC TITLE:	1989	1990	1991	1992	1993	TOTAL

PRIORITISING WILL:
GIVE YOU CONTROL OVER YOUR PREPARATION ENSURING THAT YOU WORK ON THE RIGHT AREAS, IN THE RIGHT WAY, AT THE RIGHT TIME.
HELP YOU DEVELOP YOUR OWN LUCK.
'GEAR UP' YOUR POSITIVE SUCCESS CYCLE. ALLOW YOU TO USE TIME MORE EFFECTIVELY.

Read through the first paper, (1989) listing the title of the major topic involved in each question in the topic column and a tick (✔) under 1989. Repeat the exercise for subsequent papers, before totalling the number of appearances in the last column. An additional technique is to have wider columns which allow the specific area of each topic to be noted.

DIVISION ONE: The topic will be a part of performance

DIVISION TWO: The topic very likely to be a part of performance

DIVISION THREE: The topic may be a part of performance

DIVISION FOUR: The topic might be a part of performance but less probable

EXAMPLE OF AN ANALYSIS SHEET FOR IB BUSINESS STUDIES
Grade priorities into four divisions:

KNOWLEDGE TOPICS	82	83	84	85	86	87	88	89	90
Costs Concepts	✓✓	✓							
Probability: Dec. Trees	✓DT	✓DT	✓DT	✓DT	✓PROB			✓DT	✓DT
Normal Distributions	✓	✓					✓		
Capital Appraisal Budget	✓	✓					✓		
Cost/Prod. Decision Making	✓✓								
Final A/C's	✓	✓	✓	✓					✓✓
Final A/C Anaylsis			✓✓	✓				✓✓	✓✓

PERSONAL PRIORITISING

Prioritising topics personally, as well as technically, allows students to see the syllabus in a different light – through their own eyes and according to their own feelings. If this knowledge is used in conjunction with their self assessment rating (Planning Stage, page 68) individual students can better appreciate the work ahead of them, as well as being able to recognise some of the personal problems with which they will have to cope during the rest of preparation.

Personal prioritising employs the same four divisions but uses different scales for grading:

Very Easy	Easy	Difficult	Very Difficult
Very Enjoyable	Enjoyable	Unpleasant	Very Unpleasant

Recognising which areas are easy and enjoyable, and which are difficult or 'a drag', is very important when developing your personal route map.

YOUR PERSONAL ROUTE MAP

The information gained from prioritising the syllabus in terms of performance probability and personal preferences should be used to plan the detail of a student's own personal route map, and their own coping strategies, which may become necessary as final performance draws near.

Prioritising the syllabus in terms of performance probability is a technique used by sports coaches who watch videos of future opponents in order to predict likely performance patterns when their players meet. Personal prioritising allows students to become aware of their feelings for different sections of the syllabus.

The first technique emphasises those parts of the syllabus most likely to be a part of a student's performance, which therefore should take up a large portion of preparation time. The second allows a student control over downgrading, or even jettisoning altogether, some areas of the syllabus in order to be better able to cope with the problems of their own preparation as it progresses. Isn't this dangerous? Don't examination boards increasingly try to examine the whole syllabus? Yes, they do, for example:

> Rolf Schroder, Principal of Davies, Laing and Dick, who has been advising candidates for over thirty years, said: 'Fifteen years ago you could predict questions – now you can't. You can say which subjects must be covered. You can say some parts of the curriculum are more important than others. But the increasing tendency for examiners to use multiple-choice questions means you have to have a broad general knowledge of the syllabus. You might, for example, predict there is going to be a question on A. You mug up every aspect of A. Then, on the day of the exam, a question comes up: 'Compare A with B' – if you know nothing about B you are stumped.

But, remember the words of the Chief Examiner quoted on page 13: 'Some parts of the syllabus are so important that they have to be examined.' There is always a probability pattern. This is true of all performance situations; some segments of every game will always be present – tennis matches will always contain services, rugby matches scrums, soccer and hockey games 2 v 1 situations.

Your analysis of past exam papers should enable you to see which questions are most likely to be a part of your performance. Situations which are 'always' a part of performance are the ones to practice first and most often. If they are prepared properly, a performer will become really confident about major sections of their performance: in a sense it is almost 'as if' they have been given the answers in advance of the exam.

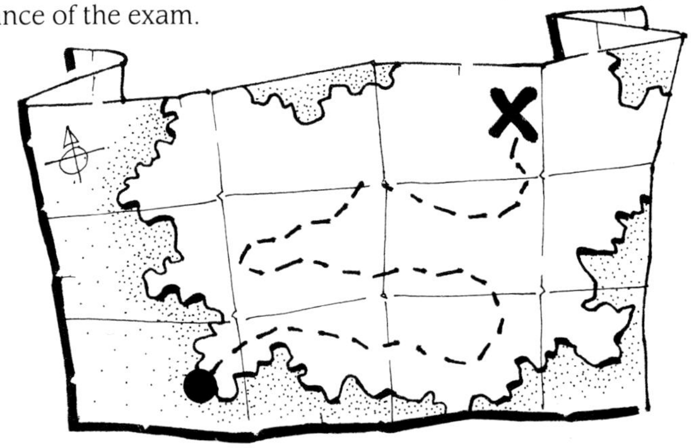

YOU ARE NOW READY TO DEVELOP YOUR PERSONAL ROUTE MAP
No plan can begin anywhere but the beginning; no journey can be travelled but by small stages. It is the experience of travelling the journey by which the traveller gains. Each step the traveller makes will increase their power as a performer.

WRITING THE PERFORMANCE SCRIPT IS A HANDS-ON EXPERIENCE

Your Performance Script serves the same purpose as an actor's script when rehearsing a play, or a musician practising a score of music. Writing the Performance Script from notes, handouts, texts, course work, abbreviated so that it is easy and quick to use, understand and memorise, is one of the most important tasks of preparation. The time spent on this task represents a 'huge investment' in your future performance.

WRITING THE PERFORMANCE SCRIPT

Is a 'hands on' experience. You are the only person involved: it is you who is physically writing it.	Will give you: A feeling of control over the body of knowledge.
Will occupy a lot of time. It may therefore involve sacrificing other activities which might have to be temporarily curtailed.	An easing of anxiety arising from the progress made. A major chunk of work is behind you.
Will be physically hard work!	A feeling of achievement which will give a big boost to Your Self Confidence

UNLESS THIS FOUNDATION IS LAID SOLIDLY AND PURPOSEFULLY, LITTLE FURTHER PROGRESS WILL BE POSSIBLE, AND THE CUMULATIVE PROCESS OF DEVELOPMENT WILL ABRUPTLY STOP!

STEP 1 – PRESENTATION

SHOULD YOU USE CARDS OR PAPER?

The answer to this question should be one of personal choice, provided that it is made on the basis of reliable information. Both methods of presentation have their advantages and disadvantages:

a) Presentation of Script on Cards

Advantages
- Cards are small in size Convenience – easy to carry
- Can be carried in pockets
- Can be carried with person at all times
- Cheapness

Disadvantages
- Cards are too small Not good if writing is large
- Insufficient space means organisation is cramped
- May be too large a number to file

b) Presentation of Script on File Paper. (The best size of paper is A4

Advantages
- Paper is big enough to allow good use of space
- Paper is big enough to allow better patterning.
- Files are easy to carry around
- Files protect notes.
- Files are flexible in use – when walking, sitting in chair or at a desk.
- You still have the opportunity to abbreviate onto cards at a later stage of preparation, when your judgement of priorities is better, and when summaries of main points, formulae, quotations are more important.

Disadvantages
- Paper too big to carry around
- More bulk
- More expensive

c) Additional factors to bear in mind!

If you decide on cards
- Ensure that you have a title card at the beginning.
- Divide each section with divider cards of a different colour, which have name tabs on one end. Divide each subsection with a coloured card but without the tabs.
- Buy cards which are big enough and strong enough for the job.

If you decide on files
- 1½ ring files are best for the purpose. They are large enough to contain all the information, but small enough to be carried and used easily. Do not use either 4" files or envelope files. The former is too big and clumsy, the latter does not allow you to flick quickly through the index of your knowledge.
- Use coloured divider cards with name tabs.

And then there is cost!

Cost! Surely cost is not a major consideration. It may not be, gut some people may not want to go to the expense. But, even if it is a consideration, be generous – treat yourself to the best. The return on your investment will be good.

EXAMPLE: LAKESIDE PRINTING LTD

The printers of this book began life in a wooden hut at the bottom of a country garden, but have now expanded to two premises, one with a street frontage. Visiting the plant one day, I noticed a recently purchased machine which looked very expensive. 'You must be doing very well', I said, 'how much did this piece of machinery cost?' 'Over £75,000 replied the owner, 'expensive yes, but if you are going to live in these premises for 10 hours a day, you might as well buy the best equipment with which to work. It is much easier and makes the quality of life much more satisfying.'

WHICH TO USE

The decision should be made solely on which is the best method for YOU. In coming to a decision consider all the above information, the use of the notes will be put to, your own personal learning styles (refer to Planning Stage; Self Assessment) and the fact that if you choose paper now, the opportunity to revert to cards later in the programme is still open to you.

STEP 2: ORGANISING YOUR RESOURCES

1. COLLECT TOGETHER
Every piece of information from your course – class notes, your own notes, articles, essays, handouts, specimen notes, etc.

2. DIVIDE INFORMATION INTO MAJOR SEGMENTS OF THE SYLLABUS

3. SELECT

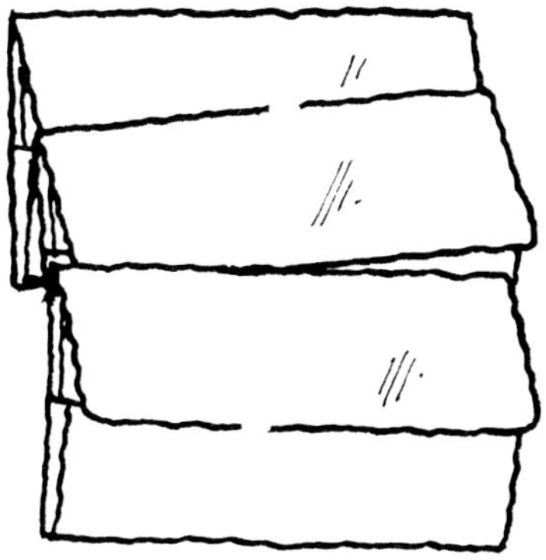

INFORMATION WITH WHICH THE PERFORMANCE SCRIPT WILL BE WRITTEN

INFORMATION TO GO IN THE SUSPENSE FILE

INFORMATION TO THROW OUT

The only information you need to keep at this stage is information essential to your Performance Script. Everything else should be thrown out. Be ruthless; you will be surprised how much paper you can bin! Make sure you enjoy the experience.

Murphey's Law (that which you throw away today you will want tomorrow) is acknowledged and controlled by having a Suspense File. Information – essays for instance – about which you are uncertain can, perhaps temporarily, be placed into a Suspense File, the purpose of which is to act as your own Reference Library. You probably won't use it often, but it is comforting to know that the information is there if required.

MAKE YOUR SCRIPT REALLY GOOD
A GOOD PERFORMANCE SCRIPT SHOULD BE:
ATTRACTIVE AND LOGICAL, EASY AND QUICK TO READ, CLEAR AND CONCISE.

STEP 3: WRITING THE ACTUAL SCRIPT

The purpose of the Performance Script is to:
1. Organise your knowledge – to answer questions better!
2. Introduce information to your memory – to encode it in the right way.

It should tell a story:

EMMA'S EXPERIENCE

Emma studied Business Studies a year or two ago. In class one day, shortly after the completion of mocks she piped up 'Mr Williams, I want to tell you something about your notes. Last term, when we were studying marketing, I used to think they were disorganised. Revising for the mocks during the holidays I read through all the notes we made last term and I found that they told a story.'
'Good', I replied 'that is exactly what they are meant to do'.
'What does that do for you?' I enquired.
'It made me feel relieved and very confident.'

When information is presented as a story, it is:
Easier to read
Easier to understand
Easier to memorise

Help your memory system by using the acronym

F I O R D S

FEED INFORMATION
Which is meaningful to you

I INTEND TO REMEMBER IT

ORGANISE IT
In a logical sequence

READABLE
Use of space, pattern colours, diagrams

DIGESTIBLE SLICES OF INFORMATION

STORYLINE
Link information into to read like a story (connections are important to your memory)

THE ART OF SELECTION IS THE ART OF WHAT TO LEAVE OUT

The contents should include:
NOT ALL – the knowledge in the syllabus – BUT, ALL THAT YOU WILL NEED FOR THE EXAM.

Its length should be:
Long enough to cover the major points, but short enough to maintain interest. Length is a matter of personal preference. If you are in doubt at this stage err on the side of longevity. The script can always be abbreviated further at a later stage.

LAYOUT STRUCTURE IS VERY IMPORTANT
1. Adopt a standard layout throughout the Script:

Layout is of crucial importance if the story is to be told effectively. Distinguish major segments of the syllabus with a coloured card (preferably with a tab label), and major topics in each segment by coloured paper (again with a tab label-tab labels can easily be added by use of a stapler).

Major concepts within each section should always begin on a new sheet, their title being printed in capital letters in the top right hand corner (so that they will catch the eye easily when you are flicking through the script).

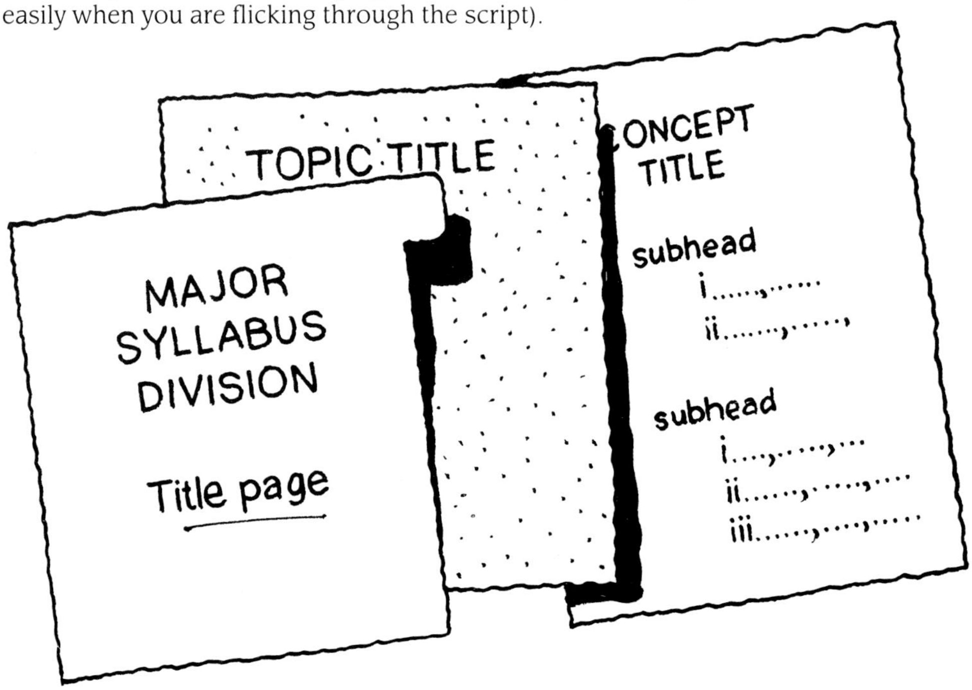

2. Write the text of the Script:
a) On one side of the paper only:
This allows the script to be re-ordered and organised at a later date if necessary (scissors and Prittstick are useful too). Additional information can be inserted, without the rest of the script being disturbed.

It is less tiring for the muscles of the eye, neck and shoulders to read down a page vertically, rather than repeatedly across horizontally, which would be the case if the script was written using both sides of the paper.

b) Using the middle of the page:
Just as the script as a whole has a standard format, so too should each page. Use the left hand side of each page for headings, the middle of each page for main points and the right hand side for detail.

The eye uses less energy to do:

'this' than 'this'

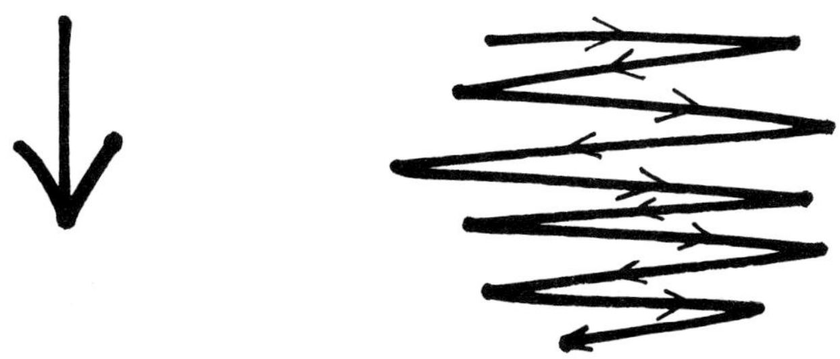

The eye takes in whole pieces of information at or around a point: eyes use more energy if the pattern moves horizontally backwards and forwards.
Example
The sentence:

'The man walked to the beach and saw hundreds of people swimming.'

is presented better like this:

'The man walked to the beach and saw hundreds of people
swimming'.

than this:

"The man walked to the beach and saw hundreds of people
swimming'.

ORGANISING AND PRESENTING DETAIL

Detail can be presented in many different ways, all of which have their own advantages and disadvantages (a range of ideas is included below and in the toolbox). The decision on which method to use should take into account the personal preferences of a student, but should be made chiefly on which method best serves 'the purposes of the Performance Script.

A STRONG RECOMMENDATION AT THIS STAGE: USE THE LINEAR METHOD. For example:

*1 SUBHEADS	**2 MAJOR POINT	***3 TITLE/KEY WORD	TITLE ****4 POINT OF DETAIL
A. 1st MAJOR SUBHEAD			
	i.	Title Word/Key Word	– point of detail
	ii. 2nd	Title Word	– detail 1, detail 2. Eg: example to supp
B. 2nd MAJOR SUBHEAD			
	1.	Title Word/Key Word	– detail, commas/ dashes used to break up item

Notice that the different sections of the notes begin at standard points across the page – Major headings at *1, key label words at **2, and points of detail and supporting examples at ***3.

<u>A. ENGLISH ATTITUDES</u>

1. Pre-1872 attitude (Disrali-Crystal Palace)

    a) Indifference ⟶ positive dislike

    b) Neglect of Oz: Failure to annexe NZ

    c) Some outstanding exceptions -

    Stephen, Wakefield, Durham,
    Dilke, Gordon

MAJOR SUBHEADS

Act as signposts. They should stand out like headlines – use capitals, or underlinings.

KEY WORDS/TITLE WORDS

Act as titles for small sections of information. You may have to think carefully to create title words from the information. Make them the first word of a line: make them standout.

WHAT DETAIL?

Each section of text should contain:

- Definition of Concept/Idea
- Explanation of Concept
- Specific Techniques/Principles
- Advantages/Disadvantages, For/Against
- Opinions about the topic, concept

NO BURIED TREASURE

Do not bury important pieces of information by writing around it. Always indent to allow the title word to stand out

Layout is vital as the examples below illustrate. Example 1 is organised, formal and with a lyrical pattern demonstrating the virtues of good design. Example 2 however, although attempting to be more interesting fails to impart readily and easily the information.

Example 1

0745	Ass	Merchant Taylor's School
0800	Dpt	Merchant Taylor's School
1445	Eta	Holyhead
1545	Dpt	Holyhead via B & I Line
1915	Eta	Dublin
1945	Dpt	Dublin Docks for City
2030	Eta	Dublin Int. YH.

Example 2

depart Sevenoaks: 16 32
arrive London Bridge: 16 56
take underground Northern Line to Monument
underground: Circle Line to Liverpool Street
depart Liverpool Street: 17 55
arrive Norwich: 19 51
travel to Swanton Morley by bus. Arrive about 20 30

DIGESTIBLE PIECES

Knowledge, like food, can be taken in such a quantity that it is rejected. Breaking it into smaller sections makes it much easier to remember, eg. telephone numbers:

Would you find it easy to remember this number, 01035139735569,

There are thirteen digits in this number, it isn't very digestible, but if it is broken down into its constituent parts it becomes much easier.

010 351 39 735569

It becomes even easier if each sub group is labelled:

010 = International dialling code
351 = Portugal
39 = Coimbra
735569 = subscriber's number

And, if you dial Portugal regularly the only part you would really have to 'try' to remember would be 735569 the other parts being already grooved into your memory.

THE MAGIC FIVE

Group information in sections of no more than five points. Five is a very digestible number possibly because most of us learned to count using the fingers of our hands. The practice is deeply grooved into our memory.

USE ABBREVIATIONS

Abbreviations shorten the script without losing its clarity.

a) Examples of standard abbreviations:

n.b.	note well	fig.	figure (diagram)
i.e.	that is	loc. cit.	in the passage already quoted
e.g.	for example	infra.	below, on the following page
ad fin.	towards the end		because
ad init.	at the beginning	<	less than
c.	circa (about)	=	equal to
cf.	confer (compare)	≠	not equal to
et al	and others	∴	therefore
ibid	in the same place (same book, etc.)	>	greater than
ed.	edited by		

b) Use well-known abbreviations: – His. = History; Eng. = English; Bio. = Biology.

c) Use vertical or horizontal lists.

d) Never write sentences – use only phrases, and cut out verbs, prepositions etc.

e) Use your own shorthand:

U = you	↗ = increase
2 = to	↘ = decrease
4 = for	→ = leads to

OTHER PRESENTATION TECHNIQUES TO INCORPORATE

Hook Ups

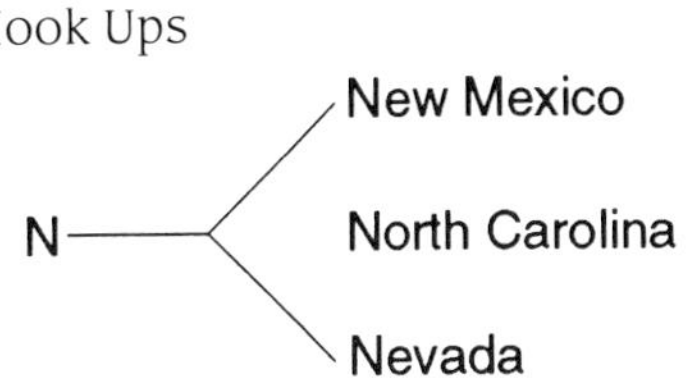

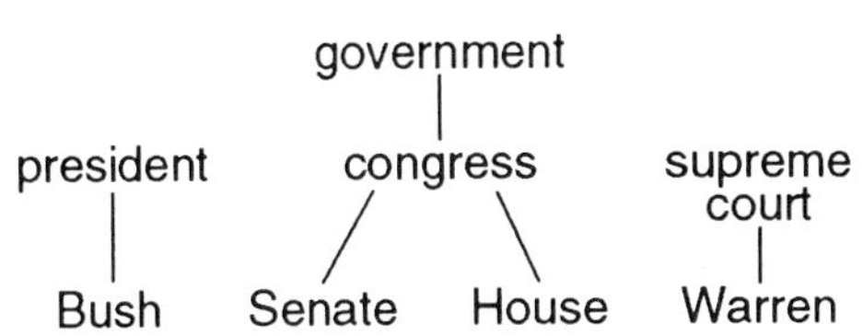

Visual Chains

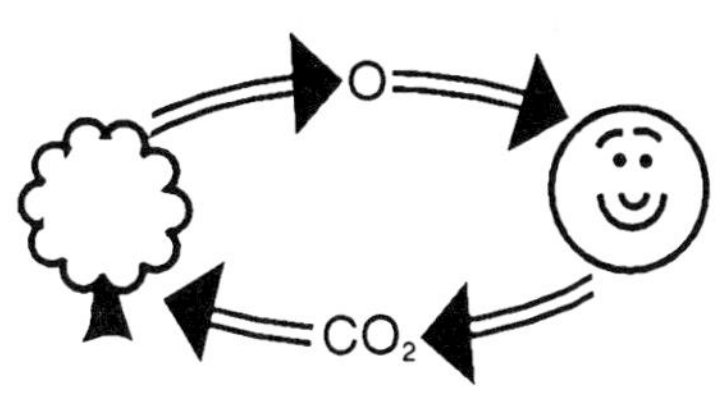

Time Lines

1789	1854	1871	1929
French Revolution	Crimean War	Unification of Germany	Wall Street Crash

Flow Charts

Clock Patterns

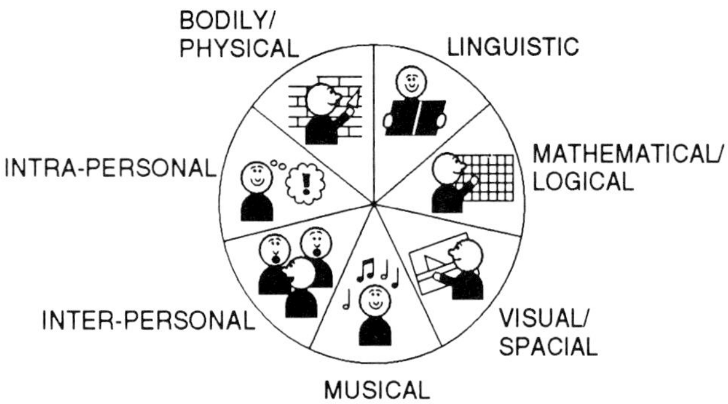

Chain Links

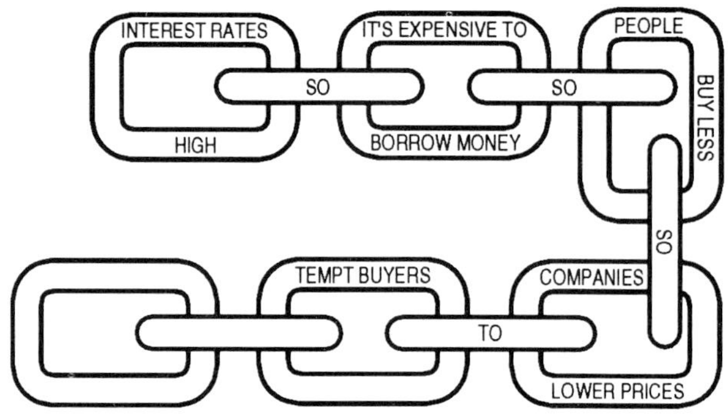

WHERE TO START?

A start can be made in a number of places:
At the part of a syllabus studied first – then follow on sequentially.
At the part of the syllabus you find easiest.
At the part of the syllabus you find most difficult.
At Division 1 subjects, then two, then three.
At the part of the syllabus you find most interesting; the part you find least interesting.

It doesn't matter where you start, so long as:
YOU DO
YOU START ON TIME
YOU ENSURE THERE IS A LOGICAL PATTERN

SHOULD THE PERFORMANCE SCRIPT BE LEARNT AT THIS STAGE?

NO!

DO NOT START TO MEMORISE THE SCRIPT NOW!
If the Script is memorised now it has to be retained in the memory system for two months. Research suggests that the average adult cannot remember 50% of what they read only a few minutes after. Twenty four hours later, recall reduces to 20 per cent.

MEMORY WORKS BEST WHEN . . .
It is fed with digestible pieces.
The information becomes familiar – is 'grooved' over time.

LEAVE MEMORISATION UNTIL THE LEARNING STAGE

STAGE 3

FAMILIARISATION

INTRODUCTORY THEMES

The overall goal of the Familiarisation Stage is to develop the student into a powerful and self confident performer.

The Performance Scripts (written during the Organisation Stage) are central; they are the vehicle by which this change and development will be achieved. By using them to answer questions, write essays and review knowledge, the student becomes increasingly familiar with the whole script – its layout, organisation and the detail of knowledge: by using them to perform practice examinations the student becomes increasingly familiar with the performance situation.

THE MORE ACTIVE YOUR PROGRAMME THE GREATER WILL BE YOUR ENJOYMENT AND SATISFACTION.

Quite obviously, practice is a crucial part of the familiarisation process. Important though it is however, other tasks – struggling to discover for yourself, grooving your memory and the integration of all your performance skills in advance of actual performance – are important also.

FAMILIARISATION MEANS "DISCOVERING FOR YOURSELF"
Development involves change; change involves struggle and self discovery. Often these processes involve making mistakes – and there is nothing wrong with this! Mistakes, a vital part of the learning process, occur because we are striving to achieve – and that is precisely when learning starts to happen.

WE MAKE NOTHING, IF WE DO NOT MAKE MISTAKES.

Don't worry about mistakes – the Familiarisation Stage is the place to make them! Accept them and use them for your own ends.

FAMILIARISATION HELPS TO GROOVE YOUR MEMORY
Although the Familiarisation Stage does not require full recall, it is very important for the memorisation process as a whole. When your memory is fed information a piece at a time, a little every day – a process known as 'The Drip Effect' – very quickly and easily, it becomes familiar with the body of knowledge. 'Grooving' this knowledge deeply into the memory paths of your long term memory, helps its storage which makes retrieval and recall mush easier.

Learning the Performance Script can often be left until the next stage of the programme, but some students may prefer to start memorising during the Familiarisation Stage.

Here are some activities which will help your memory:

1. Using your Performance Script constantly, to find answers to problems posed during practice sessions.
2. Reorganising your Performance Script:
   a) Make the Script more visual
   Produce flow charts and clock patterns to re-express information in a visual way.
   Colour Code section of notes with highlighters.
   Add Learning Maps which summarise whole sections on a single page

b) Summarise the Script still further:
Abbreviate particular sections.
Make associations/connections between ideas, definitions, concepts, principles, theories, etc.

and

thoughts that are:

comical
odd

rude
sexual

bizarre
interesting

Any one of these connections will make the information more memorable and personal – and therefore easier to recall.

c) Visualise what you are learning:
'A picture is worth a thousand words' is an old saying and a true one.

d) Transfer the Script:
to Performance Cards
to Poster-size Learning Maps pinned to the wall
to Poster-size Flow Charts pinned to the wall

All research on memory suggests that the single most important activity is constant and regular 'review' which becomes even more powerful if it is:

KEEP USING YOUR PERFORMANCE SCRIPT TO ANSWER QUESTIONS

Multi-Sensory Review

- Reading the information
- Speaking it aloud
- Picturing it
- Selecting one or two key words
- Physically writing them down

Constant familiarisation will make recall much easier – and it can at least double your success.

% of time reading	% of time spent on review	Av. No. of syllables remembered
100%	0%	65
80%	20%	92
60%	40%	98
40%	60%	105
20%	80%	137

WARNING: IF YOU GROOVE YOUR MEMORY WRONGLY YOU WILL HAVE TO DEPROGRAMME BEFORE FEEDING IN NEW INFORMATION

EXAMPLE:

There is a suburb of Brussels called Boitsfort. When English people first come across this name, they often pronounce it 'Boytsfort'. I did this, and when, two years later, I discovered the correct pronunciation – Bwafort – my memory was so grooved with the original that I had a very hard job re-programming my memory.

Bad habits are difficult to change once they have become a part of your grooved memory.

FAMILIARISATION MEANS 'INTEGRATING PERFORMANCE SKILLS'
Your final performance requires the integration of four skills – technical, organisation, physical and mental. Unless these skills are practised within the same kind of environment you will experience during final performance, and unless you, the only person who will be performing in the exam room, practise integrating them until they become second nature, you cannot say that you have prepared to the best of your ability.

FAMILIARISATION HELPS SELF CONFIDENCE
Too often we focus on our weaknesses, on the work we haven't yet done, or the topic we still cannot understand. So much so that we don't notice our successes. If your struggle to achieve seems stuck on amber, remember your successes – link them to the Success Cycle and your positive self talk.

WHERE TO START? HOW TO PROCEED?
You can start at any point in the syllabus, but it would be advisable to be guided by the results of your prioritising.

Proceed methodically through the high priority areas of each of your syllabi. Maintain the areas in which you are already strong, but enhance the areas which require more work.

If there are still some areas causing you major distress by the time Familiarisation ends, you might have to consider jettisoning them in order to develop performance coping strategies.

MAINTAIN YOUR PERFORMANCE ROUTINE
Routines have to be practised – like everything else. If it works for you maintain the Performance Routine you adopted in the Organisation Stage. If you have had difficulty with it, analyse why and change it. Once you are happy, make it a part of every work and practice session.

A WORK ROUTINE DURING FAMILIARISATION

1. SELECT A QUESTION

2. READ THE QUESTION
   Underlining key words
   Check – technical words
   Check – instructional words / messages

3. QUESTION THE QUESTION
   What concept(s) are involved?
   What techniques are involved?
   Which part of the Performance Script will be needed?

4. USE THE PERFORMANCE SCRIPT
   Look up the correct section of the script.
   Select major and minor points.
   Formulate answer in your mind (mental rehearsal).

5. THINKING/PLANNING
   Thinking time – on paper.
   Doodle if you need to on rough paper.
   Plan answer.

6. **WRITE ANSWER**
   a) Write our answer in full if it is a calculation question.
   b) Write our answer in draft if it is an essay
7. **HAND IN**
8. **RECEIVE BACK**
   Analyse, question, assess, redo/or/smile!

ROUTINE WHEN FACING QUESTIONS

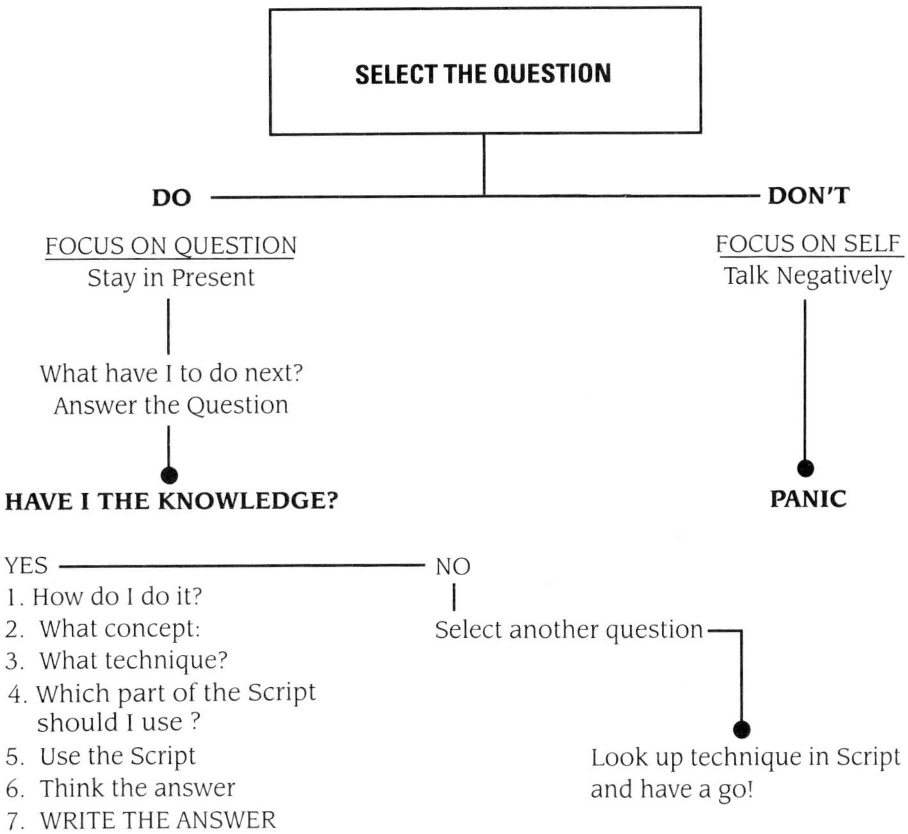

THE RULES OF THE GAME

SUCCESSFUL PEOPLE MAKE A HABIT OF DOING WHAT UNSUCCESSFUL PEOPLE DON'T LIKE TO DO

If achievement and pride are important, then the first question you ask before playing any game is "what are the rules?" because if you don't know the rules you won't know how to play the game to your advantage. If the challenge is important enough, you won't be satisfied with performing "anyway" you will make sure that you "perform absolutely the right way". Understanding the 'Rules of the Game' enables you to have more control over your problem solving making it more successful and more enjoyable.

THE RULES OF THE EXAM GAME ARE:

RULE 1

BEHAVE LIKE A WINNER IN PREPARATION AND PERFORMANCE

RULE 2

SELECT THE BEST QUESTIONS FOR YOU:
READ ALL THE MESSAGES IN THE QUESTION

RULE: 3

LAY THE FOUNDATIONS OF YOUR ANSWER WELL

RULE 4

ANSWER THE QUESTIONS THE WAY THE EXAMINER WANTS, NOT THE WAY YOU WANT

RULE 5

EXAMINERS ARE FRIENDS: KEEP THEM THAT WAY

RULE I

Research by Jim Lowhr on a large number of international tennis champtions suggests that there are common behavioural characteristics distinguishing 'winners' from 'losers'. The behaviours associated with winners are:

WINNERS' BODY LANGUAGE IS POSITIVE:
Erect, looking ahead, alert

WINNERS REACT POSITIVELY TO WHATEVER HAS HAPPENED:
An acceptance of what 'is' and their ability to cope with it.

WINNERS MAINTAIN PHYSICAL COMPOSURE:
They recognise the need for relaxation to regain their composure

WINNERS REMAIN ALERT AND FOCUSED ON THE PRESENT:
Being positive is a physical thing as well as a a cognitive thing. As in the Success Cycle if you practise behaving like a winner there is a greater chance that you will think like one, and be one.

RULE 2

Exam questions are examples of communication systems.

THE SENDER (The Examiner) → sends a message to (the question) → A RECEIVER (the student)

and then receives 'feedback' from the student in the form of a written answer

Communication systems are simple in outline, yet communication failures, the result either of the sender or the receiver, or a combination of the two, occur very frequently. They will occur in the exam unless students practise controlling those areas of the system which are under their control.

1. Read questions slowly, deliberately and physically.
Highlight or underline key concepts and phrases.
Extract key phrases onto rough paper.

2. Don't have expectations of words in a question.
This is a common cause of communication breakdown made by everyone at some point in their life. For instance, for many years I thought the name of this chemist was NELSON WINGATE, simply because the name Nelson has been engrained in my memory from a very early age. When I saw a name which was similar, I expected to see Nelson – and so I did.

Melson
Wingate

This communication barrier is so common that some manufacturers even use it to try to persuade customers to buy their goods, as can be seen from the illustration below. Take a quick glance at the number and see what number you see:

£1,000.00 CASH JACKPOT

Do you see £1 million or £1 thousand? Clever use of space and punctuation lead the reader to 'think' it is £1 million. Insure against such expectations by 'talking yourself' through each question deliberately, carefully, slowly.

3. Converse with the Examiner – get onto the same wavelength.
Examiners use technical language (jargon specific to the subject) when designing questions. During familiarisation practice using the same vocabulary.

This should not be a difficult habit to acquire. In many social situations we try to speak in language we think will appeal to the other person. Do it in exams too.

4. 'Ask the right questions: you will get the right answers'.

Students need to ask two types of questions:

BUT WHAT ARE THE RIGHT QUESTIONS? RUDYARD KIPLING HAD AN ANSWER. HE WROTE:
'I KEEP SIX HONEST SERVING MEN,
(THEY TAUGHT ME ALL I KNEW):
THEIR NAMES ARE WHAT AND WHY AND WHEN
AND HOW AND WHERE AND WHO?'

TECHNICAL QUESTIONS
Deal with knowledge, concepts and ideas.

ASK:
What concept is being asked?
Do I understand this concept?
What are the key technical words/ phrases in the question?

Which part of the Performance Script is relevant?

Are there any 'bunkers' involved?
Golf courses designers include bunkers at a hole to make it more fun or more of a challenge. Some exam questions use the same technique.

Questions which might be too simple are deliberately made more interesting by the inclusion of specific pieces of qualifying information. Golfers avoid bunkers by recognising their existence, selecting the right club and by using the right technique. Students should do the same. Look out for bunkers, and cope with them by treating them correctly.

What opportunities does the question offer to allow me to display additional knowledge? eg: diagrams, graphs, fieldwork, examples, case studies, quotations, etc.

INSTRUCTIONAL QUESTIONS
State what you are being asked to do.

ASK:
What is the question asking me to do?
eg: define, contrast, compare, outline, assess, examine, consider, brief = select, key factors = select, for one country/ in one economy = factual support/examples from a specific area.

Are there any instructional messages in the question? eg: with the aid of diagrams, satisfactory, consider the extent, are influenced by . . . Such phrases are crucially important. They focus your attention more precisely by qualifying, refining and directing you to select more specific areas of knowledge and technique.

Even when a question does not pose a question, turn it into one.

eg: Define democracy can become
What is democracy?

5. Select questions which offer you the best opportunity.
Consider both types of message. Do you understand:

- What knowledge is required?
- How the question wants you to use the knowledge?

What percentage of the marks can you achieve on this question?

- Marks signify the relative importance of question. The mark distribution should be taken into account when deciding which questions to attempt, particularly when selecting the last or next to last question.

Have you enough time to achieve this percentage mark?

6. Never overlook gifthorses
Too often students dismiss questions which look too simple, too straightforward, or carry only a small number of marks. Don't overlook such questions. They play the same role as 'A Starter for Ten' did in the TV show Univervity Challenge; They allow you to start and they increase your confidence.

RULE 3

1. Build the foundations before you start to write.
Write the answers the way builders build houses – the foundations first, then the structure, add the stylish interesting parts and finally give a conclusion, the equivalent of a builder's 'topping out' ceremony! This might sound boring to some. It might be too, but it is 'the right behaviour'. Think and plan – before you write. Without foundations a house will crumble; it is the same with an answer. Just as the foundations of a building are built below ground where nobody sees them, the foundations of an answer are written on rough paper.

2. Inject control into your answers
Students often feel that they are controlled by examiners. This is sometimes true, but not always. If a student clearly states the assumptions they have made at the outset, better control of time and selection is possible. The examiner is also able to see that the writer is actively involved in understanding the question, rather than just being a passive respondent.

3. Make the examiner 'feel good' about you.
In higher level examinations (A Level and above) the impression an examiner gains of the student – sometimes called 'impression marking' – is an important element of the examination procedure. Your answer, and the way it is presented, should be used to create a favourable impression of you, not just as a student, but as a person. Your personal qualities can be very significant. Examiners are impressed, within the first paragraphs, by organisation, control, positiveness, and the pace of the writing.

Inject your work with:

Clarity
Organise and pattern the answer into sections.

Patience
Allow time to answer a section before moving onto the next.

Care
Give examples, allow time for checkpoints, give signposts when the answer moves on.
Correct spelling, particularly of subject jargon is important. What kind of impression do you think you create when, after two years study, the word Business is spelled Buisness?

Discipline
Maintain progress along your chosen route map without being distracted down side alleys.

Persistence
Maintain your determination to follow a route to its conclusion.

Decision Making
Allows you to control information rather than information controlling you.

If you doubt this advice, consider the following A Level Business Studies question.:

EXAMPLE: 'A LEVEL BUSINESS STUDIES QUESTION – Stock Valuation

> Question: When charging materials to either process or job, stock control involves recording purchases and issues of materials and valuing stock-on-hand, on a consistent basis. Assuming a system of 'First-in, First-out', compute the cost of each issue and the value of final stock, from the following date.
>
> The Chief Examiner commented:
> By far the easiest question on the paper and yet not that many candidates attempted. This must call into question the question answering strategies of candidates. Those who attempted it found the marks easy to get and more must be encouraged to read the whole paper (and the whole of individual questions) carefully before attempting any one question.
> Again an ordered answer is the best way to success and many candidates throw marks away because their answer is not structured. It is not that there are marks for structure but rather that lack of structure leads to errors or failure to take all matters into account and therefore to wrong answers:

Quite often, questions challenge more than just technical skills. Sometimes too, technical skills are deliberately minimised in order to highlight personal qualities, as the Chief Examiner's report above illustrates.

4. Don't straitjacket yourself; retain a wide focus

Students often rush into a question and answer it with much too narrow a focus. 'The Inverted Pyramid' model will help you retain a wide focus.

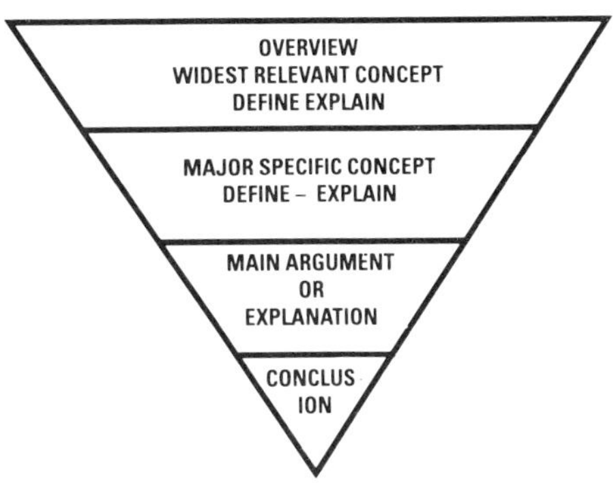

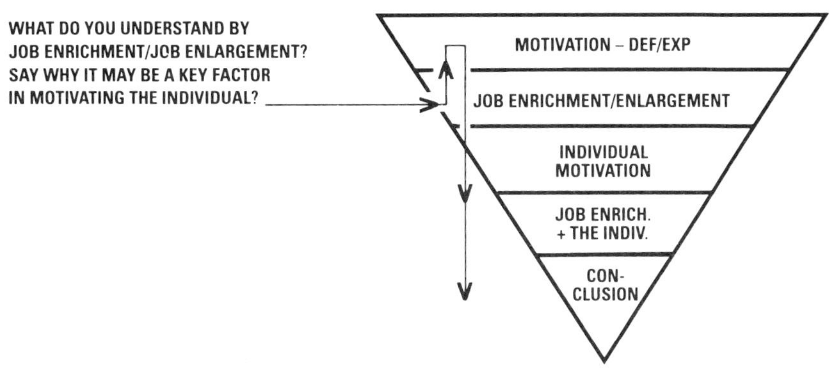

The Inverted Pyramid should be used when thinking through and planning an answer. It reminds you to think 'as widely as necessary' about the concepts and ideas in the question, before progressively narrowing to a precise conclusion.

The technique can also be used when a question focuses on a specific part of a topic rather than on the topic as a whole. If you focus narrowly, you will miss the opportunity to show how much knowledge you have. In such a case, the pyramid will remind you of the context of the question, as well as allowing you to revisit the concept, before proceeding with an answer to the specific question.

5. Decide the correct starting place.
Once the correct starting position is known, it is easier to organises your answer logically by developing a route map. Different types of question have different starting points.

TYPE OF QUESTION:	STARTING PLACE:
Essays:	A Definition of major concept followed by brief explanation of relevance to essay title.
Short Structured Questions:	Definition, a brief explanation and supporting examples
Analysis Questions:	Start patterning information on rough paper. Analyse by asking questions of the information. Develop criteria by which to make a judgement.
Mechanical/Quantitative Questions:	Select the right technique. Organise your answer by either numbered sections or an organisation chart before writing in any numbers.

6. 'Overkill' but K.I.S.S.
The principle of 'overkill' can be used in short structured answers, worth between 1 - 5 marks, to prevent students rushing on too fast, with too narrow a focus, thereby missing opportunities to gain marks. To make certain of gathering all available marks make at least 5 hard informative statements, supported by detail and examples.

Overkill holds one danger: swamping the reader with irrelevant information. K.I.S.S. 'Keep it Simple Stupid!' prevents this by using 'the Layering Technique' to control information into a relevant pattern. For example:

Define the concept
Explain the concept
Support the explanation
Give examples

RULE 4

Examiners expect formal responses expressing:

1. KNOWLEDGE
Understanding and logical use of concepts

2. CONTROL
Of the question that is on the paper not the one in the mind of the student, of knowledge that is relevant, and of time.

3. EXPRESSION
Which should be precise, selective and relevant.
Higher level examinations, (A Levels and above) do not regard skills of recall as highly as those of interpretation, explanation and analysis.

The advice of a history examiner should be borne in mind: 'Before putting pen to paper, candidates might remember that the very best scripts are almost invariably a little short of average length, rather than grossly in excess of it.'

'How you say it' and 'how you use what you know' is every bit as important as 'what you know.'

This might appear obvious when written down in black and white, yet, just as some people find it difficult to conform to socially acceptable modes of dress and behaviour, some students find it difficult to give examiners what they want in the way they want – despite the fact that they have the knowledge. Rather than answer questions the way examiners expect, students too often write in the way they want, as is illustrated by the example below.

Example:
A QUESTION ON MARKETING. Using your knowledge of the marketing environment suggest why smoking appears to be in decline?

Answer received:
'Prices are up, promotion of cigarettes is restricted, the media are publishing more and more statistics proving that smoking is a cause of lung cancer. Smoking has become socially unacceptable in some circumstances, especially at meal times. Peer pressure plays an important part.'

Answer wanted:
The concept involved is the Market Environment. This has four different segments each of which play a part in persuading people that smoking is harmful to their health. The most important factors (which could form the basis for an essay plan) are:

Economic factors
Tax, price, distribution of spending, elasticity of demand.

Political & Legal
Health Warnings, banning of smoking advertisements, increase of non smoking areas, etc.

Technological
Medical research.

Cultural
Now unfashionable – yes, but why? Leisure, Health, Fitness, Youth, Slim people are elegant, The Media etc.

The specific information given by the student above could have been organised differently to better illustrate both formal concepts and the supporting detail of the answer. Examination answers require theoretical knowledge before common sense and opinion.

SO, DON'T LET THIS HAPPEN TO YOU. WORK SMARTER, REMEMBER – BECOME CONCEPT ORIENTATED!

1. Be explicit not implicit

Ensure that the words which express your answer in an examination are explicit – clearly understood at once. The examiner cannot telephone you to ask supplementary questions like, 'what did you mean precisely when you said . . .' and as a history examiner has stated: 'Your examiner will not know you. The impression gained of your qualities as a historian will derive exclusively from what you write in the examination room.'

2. Follow through

Remember to 'follow through'. When you make assertions, support them with supporting evidence, when you make causal statements, remember that there will be effects from these causes. Don't leave the examiner hanging in mid air; follow through!

3. Insurance policies are worthwhile

Insurance policies guard against the consequences of specific risks (travel insurance is not taken out unless the person is travelling on holiday). Three types of risk occur during an exam performance:

Forgetting knowledge
Confusing knowledge
Being imprecise with knowledge

Insurance policies which guard against such risks should be devised. Being closely related to your memory they are necessarily personal, often idiosyncratic, sometimes juvenile but always sympathetic to your learning style. Here are some examples:

Scientists:
use pictorials or diagrams to help their memory rather than words.

Geographers
use a play on words to distinguish stalacmites from stalagtites. 'The mites go up, but the tites come down.'

Mathematicians:
use the vertical line of the letter Y to remind them that it is the vertical axis of a graph which is labelled Y.

Economists:
use lower case letters and arrows to distinguish the correct part of the formula of elasticity of demand.

$$\text{Elasticity of Demand} = \frac{\text{\% change in deman}d\uparrow}{\text{\% change in }p\downarrow\text{rice}}$$

Business Students:

use the association of debentures, abbreviated to 'Debs' to remind them that it is a high % of debentures relative to equity which signifies a company having high gearing.

Debentures – debs are associated with
Debs = debutantes who come from High Society

4. Solve the problem in the Examiner's time, not yours.
Exam answers have to be written in a specified time. This may seen unfair but it is not; it is simply another element of performance which has to be accepted. In other fields, formula one racing drivers have to accept that it is not the fastest driver who wins races, but the one who crosses the finishing line first. Sprinters too have to accept that the man who wins the 100 metres sprint is not necessarily the fastest sprinter, but the man who slows down the least. Controlling time and pace is a known and acknowledged element of both performance and preparation.

RULE 5

Exam performances are formal. There is a prescribed mode of behaviour which students must learn and practice otherwise they will not impress on the day.

1. Examiners are always right.
Stay in the present. The questions are what they are, not what you might wish them to be. Never argue with the question, or answer back to the Examiner. Look for opportunities to show your abilities.

2. Examiners are human beings who are already on your side: keep them there
Consider the words of one history examiner: 'the candidate might consider the psychological effect of unpacking a fresh batch of scripts all of which run to five or six supplementary answer sheets . . . what is three hours work for the candidate becomes multiplied two or three hundred times for the examiner, three or four weeks work in high summer.'

Write organised answers – clearly, carefully and logically.

If your writing is small – write larger, spreading the words out
If your words run together – write on alternate lines
If your writing is upright – slope the words to the right
If you write with light ink – use black or very dark ink

Organise numerical answers into logical sections, the answer to each section, as well as the final answer being either highlighted or underlined.

If you are unsure of a question, politely raise queries with the examiner by making and stating your assumptions.

Eg. A well planned and organised answer.

QUESTION 1

1) a) Factors which determine the return above base rate include:-

1) The opportunity cost - of initial outlay over the period.

2) The expected fluctuation in interest rates over the period. The rate presently used to calculate NPV may change during the period, affecting the calculations, and reducing the real income.

3) I.R.R. (explained below)

BUY OPTION (calculated in £'s at 10% p.a.)

Initial outlay		(100,000)
YR.1	20,000 x 0.909 =	181,180
YR.2	30,000 x 0.826 =	24,780
YR.3	30,000 x 0.751 =	22,530
		228,490
Add Residual Value	25,000 x 0.031 =	15,775
		244,165

WHAT TO DO IN THE FAMILIARISATION STAGE?

Whatever you do during the Familiarisation Stage should be performance orientated. Practice routines should be used to enhance confidence in your performance skills, to strengthen weaknesses, while still maintaining areas in which you already feel secure. Training and practice should place as high a priority on working to time, as 'mugging up the facts.'

PRACTICE TECHNIQUES

1. PERFORMANCE TESTS/SPEED TESTS

Performance Tests, sheets of 20+ direct questions, testing simple factual and conceptual knowledge, may be particularly useful in science and social science subjects, but can be adapted to any subject.

Eg. BUSINESS STUDIES REVISION TEST: FINAL ACCOUNTS

1. On what principles are Final Accounts compiled?

TRUE &	Realisation	Historic Cost
	Matching	Money Values
FAIR VIEW	Prudence	Going Concern
	Consistency	Double Entry

2. Realisation is a key principle because it decides:

   When a cost and a sale is realised.
   When the good arrives at factory and when they are delivered.

3. Matching then does what:

   Matches the same sales and costs to the same trading period in which they Arise in order to arrive at the correct profit figure for the period.

4. Realisation and Matching are particularly useful when:

   Credit sales and Costs   Depreciation

Answer such tests briefly, using a vertical list and abbreviations. Write at speed and if you do not know the answer, move quickly to the next question. Use these tests to reinforce familiarisation, quicken reaction time and increase recall.

DO NOT WORRY if some questions cannot be answered. Look up the answer in your Performance Script and try again another next time. Use these tests to reinforce familiarisation, quicken reaction time and increase recall. If the tests are tried against the clock they become Speed Tests. They can also be performed aloud, either singly or with a partner.

2. DEFINITION LISTS

Definition Lists use the Layering Technique to write long hand definitions and explanations, 1/2 to 3/4 of a side in length, of major concepts within the syllabus. The definition should be no more than one, two or three sentences in length, followed by a more detailed explanation, supported fully by examples.

3. 'KEY WORD' SELECTION TESTS

Using past papers and the format below, practise selecting the key words which carry the technical and instructional messages of the question.

Question Title	Key Words/Phrases
How far did the legislation of the Whigs between 1833 and 1841 succeed in overcoming the problems of the time?	Key Technical Words/Phrases: Legislation of Whigs, 1833/41 Problems of the time Key Instructional Words/Phrases: How far.....succeed in overcoming How far = % success

4. PRACTISE QUESTIONS FROM PAST PAPERS

Answering past questions will hone your technical skills within a performance ambience, but without the awesome consequences of performance outcomes. Joan Hall, a lecturer at the Cambridgeshire College of Arts and Technology suggests that 'Even in the security of your room the first reaction may be panic (help! I don't know this, it's all too difficult for me. I'm bound to fail). You will get over that – but it is better to go through the trauma at home than in the exam room.'

Instead of using valuable time writing longhand, use a draft/skeleton/ planned style. This is quicker, clearer, shorter and, most important of all, it focuses on selection and organisation without embroidery or elaboration. Such plans or draft answers quickly show where the gaps are in your knowledge and skill. Work through as many as you can and keep them for future preparation.

Draft answer

Account for the change in birth rate after 1870.

```
OVERVIEW - acts as a major signpost:

    Def: Birth rate = the number of births per '000 of pop.
    State trends of BR from 1801-1870 and on to 1901
    Highlight the major elements of the trend.

    Introduce 2 major explanations:
      a) BR declined because of intro contraception
      b) BR declined because of economic factors

BIRTH CONTROL ARGUMENT

    i. Increased use of contraception - supporting evidence
   ii. Law Suit against Mrs Bradlaugh
  iii. Growth of Leisured Classes

ECONOMIC FACTORS ACT AS A STIMULI

    i. Rise in cost of children (because of Factory Acts)
   ii. Rise in cost of children (Education Act 1870)
  iii. Growth of a Consumer Market (Opportunity Cost of
       Children)
   iv. Onset of Economic Recession and Slump after 1870.

CONCLUSION

    1st: Summarise the sense of each major argument.
    2nd: Select your conclusion
         It is more likely that BR declined because of
         economic factors than the increased use of birth
         control.
```

Practise a wide enough range of questions – a rough guide might be to practise twice as many topics as required by the exam paper – to allow choice in the examination room. Beware of 'question spotting': this is too risky. 'Topic spotting' is less risky and more reliable. And don't fall into the trap of always answering easy or friendly questions you enjoy!

ANDREW WHO TOOK HIS A LEVELS IN 1993.
'PREVIOUSLY I SPENT HOURS ON AREAS OF THE SYLLABUS I ENJOYED OR COULD DO WELL ALREADY. BY CONTINUALLY REPEATING 'SUCCESSFUL PEOPLE MAKE A HABIT . . . I KNUCKLED DOWN TO THE AREAS I DIDN'T ENJOY.'

Develop standard rituals and routines which will help reinforce learning. For instance:
ALL QUESTIONS:
Write the Exam Paper and the year at the top of page, followed by the question title (if it has one), and the major concept involved).

NUMERICAL QUESTIONS:
Answer using the correct technique. If any explanation is required use the draft style using a points system.

ESSAY QUESTIONS:
Use the draft style with a points system.

5. ROLE PLAY: BE THE EXAMINER – SET YOUR OWN QUESTIONS

There is no better way to 'get onto the same wavelength as the Examiner' than to set your own questions. 'If I was setting questions for students who had studied this syllabus, what questions would I set – and what kind of knowledge would I expect to receive?'

6. TIMED WORK

Time is such a vastly important element of exam performance that students must become familiar with its control in advance of exam day. Here are some suggestions:

Variation 1: Write answers within a standard time (30/35 min)

Variation 2: Deliberately allow yourself (say) 15 minutes thinking time, thereby reducing the time available for writing to a bare 20 minutes.

Variation 3: Simulate performance situations in which choice is made an element – either choice of title or areas of the syllabus.

Many subjects, particularly English, History and Economics, place a high importance on essay writing. Eric Evans of Lancaster University in 'History Study Skills' says 'Anyone who does not devote a considerable part of preparation to writing essays against the clock is throwing away marks'.

He recommends: 'In your short term strategy, two skills must be fully developed. The first concerns planning the essay: the second (which inevitably comes with rigorous practice) involves knowing what can be done in the available time. Your 'training' should be as much 'against the clock' as an athlete's . . . do at least one timed essay per week in the last three months of your course.'

7. PRACTICE EXAMS

Mock examinations give you experience of simulated exam conditions – they are in effect rehearsals – but are often too far from the final performance to be really useful. But there is no reason why your teachers cannot organise, individually or collectively, a practice exam for you.

If your teachers cannot do this, set aside a room for a rehearsal. Simulate as closely as possible the conditions which will be a part of your own performance – the arrangement of the room, desk and resources (paper, pens, instruments etc), the formal organisation of routine, perhaps with someone playing the role of invigilator, and in particular the silence of an examination room.

8. FORM A PERFORMANCE GROUP

Although the final performance is an individual one, much of your preparation, in particular during the Familiarisation Stage, will involve working in groups.

Forming small performance groups – between 2-6 people – can help almost all students in some way, although those whose inter-personal skills are more highly developed will gain the most. Such groups can exchange information about all manner of performance topics from basic knowledge and simple technical skills, to mental problems like anxiety, relaxation and concentration.

They allow students to reinforce what they know already, as well as learn new information from their friends rather than their teachers. They promote better understanding of confusing concepts and provide opportunities to assess, practice and review. Because they are a social as well as a work group, they allow students to realise that some of the problems they have as individuals are not as enormous as might have been supposed – concerns may be shared by many students. Most important of all – they are fun.

Checklist for setting up a Performance Group:

1. Choose students who get along together and who are all around the same performance level.
2. Arrange a meeting place and time.
   a) Inform parents in advance
   b) Use a private rather than a public place
   c) Food and beverages add fun and excitement;
3. Decide goals for the session with a time limit.
   a) Select a chairperson to be responsible for keeping the group to task
   b) Allow enough time to accomplish goals but not enough for a gossip
4. Activities:

TALK PUBLICALLY:	Through subject matter
DISCUSS:	Possible treatments of possible exam questions, common problems (a) technical (b) personal, individual performance routines and preparation plans.
ASSIGN:	Research and report tasks to individual members, previous exam experiences (good as well as bad) together with coping strategies.
TEST:	One another, either in pairs or as a group.
MAKE A LIST:	Of weak spots and agree to deal with them at the next meeting.

9. COMPETE WITH OTHER GROUPS
Performance Groups can compete against one another making the learning tasks even more enjoyable and exciting. Competitions should last one hour. The first twenty minutes are spent devising questions after which the groups toss to decide which group will compete first.

10. KEEP A QUESTION BANK
Keep a 'bank' of quality answers to past questions in a reference file. Over the period of preparation you will undoubtedly cover the majority of questions likely to be asked in your own performance.

11. LISTS OF 'BUNKERS'
Looking for 'bunkers' in questions can give you feelings of control and confidence. File lists of 'bunkers' as well as how you will treat them, alongside definitions lists and past paper questions.

HOW MUCH WORK SHOULD YOU DO

Students often ask for an indication of how much work needs to be done at this stage. It isn't possible to give one answer. So much depends on the individual student. Recent experience suggests that the hardest working students do four pieces of work per week, while a good average might be four practice answers and perhaps two or three Performance Tests.

EXAMPLE OF ONE WORK GROUP IN FAMILIARISATION: WEEK FOUR
EXPECTED WORK NORM – 16

THOSE MEMBERS OF THE GROUP EXCEEDING THE NORM	
Gillian	18
Andrew	22
Emma	23
Emma	17
Jonathon	17
Tina	19
Jan	31
Viv	28
Giles	18
Gavin	22
Rob	30

LAST WEEK'S WORK RECORD	
Gillian	+ 6
Mark	+ 6
Jan	+ 11
Khari	+ 8
Giles	+ 8
Gavin	+ 11
Rob	+ 10

WHAT IF'S: HOW TO COPE

By the time the Familiarisation Stage ends, your exam performance will be very close. It is likely that you will be beginning to feel more nervous. Some of these feelings will be caused by thoughts of the performance, some by a variety of factors over which control can be exerted now.

Here are some typical examples.

CANNOT UNDERSTAND AN AREA OF THE SYLLABUS

You don't have to know everything, only enough to perform well. Revisit your syllabus priorities to see how important the area is. If it is a Division 1 or 2 area you may well have to seek extra help, but if it has lower priority you might at this stage, consider jettisoning the area altogether.
Be positive – think of your strong areas.

I AM RUNNING OUT OF TIME

This is a prioritisation and time management problem (refer to page 58). In theory it is simple. It is in practice too, provided you are strong enough to be decisive. If you are running out of time you must re-prioritise. You cannot do everything, quite obviously. Decide what MUST be done.

TIME SEEMS TO BE RACING AWAY FROM YOU

The cause of this may be too many activities in your life or the way you visualise time inside your head. Most people visualise time horizontally:

but there are many other ways by which time can be visualised Alma visualises time running away from her like this:

I visualise time in a number of idiosyncratic ways:
Sport has always been very important in my life. Because matches were usually at a weekend, and because I looked forward to them, the weekend assumed much greater importance than weekdays – as the saying goes 'high days and holidays'. As a result I visualise a week like this:

Because the majority of my life has been spent in an academic environment, because the start of the academic year is Autumn rather than January, because the Winter Term is the longest of all and because the Summer Holidays (the holidays we all look forward to most) are the longest, I have – for as long as I can remember – visualised a year like this:

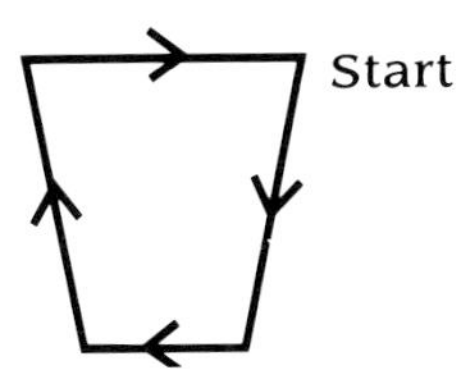

When I feel the kind of anxiety we are discussing now, I have the vivid impression of time attacking me as if I were walking into a snow storm, a situation made worse if my own self talk keeps saying: 'I've only a few minutes left' or words to that effect.

The answer is: talk to yourself slowly and deliberately and concentrate on visualising time as Alma sees it – flowing away from you, stretching out into the distance.

I AM A SLOW WRITER
Assuming that there is not any physical disability, two solutions suggest themselves.

a) Devise ways to increase your speed of writing. It may be something quite simple like changing your pen, or nib, writing on alternate lines, sloping your words in the direction of your writing so that there is greater flow and rhythm. Practice writing quicker during the Familiarisation Stage.

b) Realise that in the Final Performance you will be able to work more quickly because most of the 'thinking stage' of problem solving will already have been completed by the work you are doing now, in advance of your arrival at the exam centre.

OTHER PARTS OF MY LIFE EXERT PRESSURE ON ME?
(eg: family, parents, girl/boyfriends, etc)
Pressure from family or close friends ought to be fairly easy to deal with. Everyone has to realise that it is your performance at stake. Be decisive, tell other people the same.

If the pressure is being exerted by people a little less intimate, either drop them altogether for the duration of your preparation, or, in extremis, become incommunicado. Withdraw from everyday life: certainly take the telephone off the hook, or even go away somewhere, where no one can 'get at you.'

During my years as an 'A' Level Examiner, I had one occasion of real panic. At the same time as marking 300 exam scripts I attempted to help a friend renovate a small restaurant. The result – by the end of week one I was 80 scripts behind schedule! My answer – withdraw completely. Telling no one where I was going, I took a weekend break, at the end of which I returned completely up-to-date and, as a result of 'the change', refreshed and re-energised (check motivation on page 36).

YOU BECOME BORED, STALE OR VERY TIRED?
Stop work. Switch focus to something recreational and relaxing. Perhaps give yourself permission to take a day (or two) off. Maintain your physical well being by eating well and sleeping well – deliberately go to bed early (with a good novel perhaps).

I FALL ILL OR HAVE AN ACCIDENT?
If you fall ill, or are involved in an accident that leaves you temporarily disabled, your focus should immediately become 'getting well again'. There is nothing in life worth more than your health. When you are well enough to resume preparation, stay in the present and re-prioritise.

Exams can always be taken again, at a later date. They are not that important!

STAGE 4

LEARNING

INTRODUCTORY THEMES

Self Confidence, the attribute most sought after by any performer in whatever field, is the overall goal of the Learning Stage. By now, if you have prepared as well as we expect, your own self confidence should be quite high. The problem is maintaining it, and if possible upping it further – it is a fragile emotion, hard to gain yet so easily lost!

Control over yourself and your level of arousal, over your management of time and particularly over the sharpness and accuracy of recall of your Performance Scripts will maintain, and perhaps increase, your level of confidence in the few days remaining before final performance.

ORGANISATION OF THE LEARNING STAGE

WHY NOT INCLUDE A HOLIDAY BREAK?

Why not? You have been working hard, without a break, for nearly two months. Ahead of you is three weeks of very concentrated work. A weekend breakaway might be exactly the change of routine and focus, to bring you to a peak of preparation. A weekend is all that is being suggested – and only if it feels right to you. If it does – make it a part of your plan and go ahead – enjoy yourself!

WORK

Recall of the outline, structure and detail of your Performance Scripts is the most important activity.

WORK PERIODS

The work activities of the Learning Stage are very different to those of the Organisation and Familiarisation Stages. Then, the work was more physical than mental, now it is the other way round. Total working time should be drastically reduced to 3-5 hours in any one day, individual work periods being no longer than one hour. If they can be made shorter, they will be even more beneficial.

Recent research suggests that the first and last things you try to learn are remembered most easily. For example:

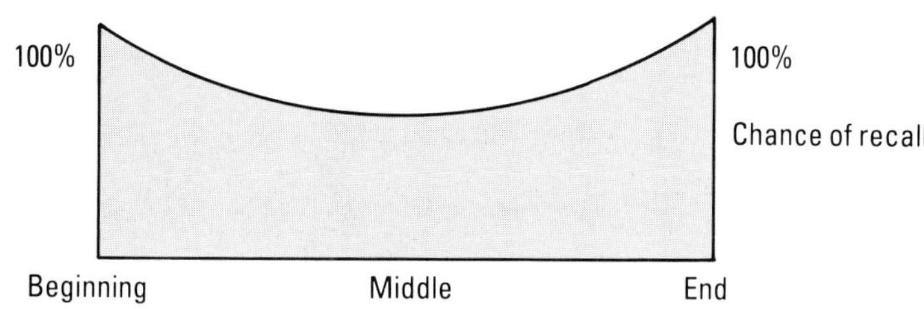

Level of recall

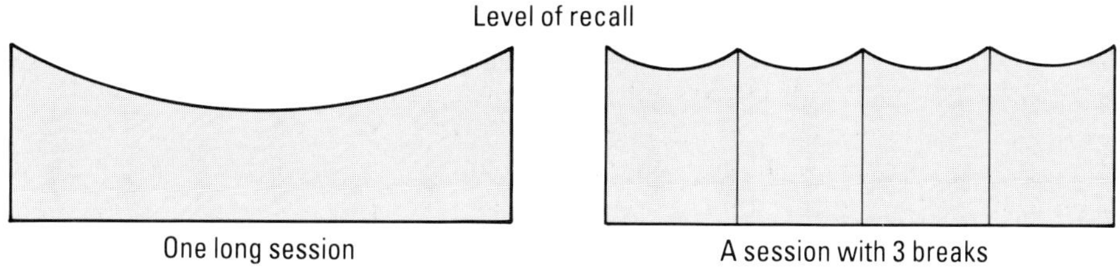

If a continuous work period is subdivided into four twenty minute sessions, with a five minute break between each, instead of there being two 'most efficient learning periods' there are eight!

Make each break a part of your work routine too. Change focus completely to look after your physical needs. Take exercise: reach above your head to stretch. This will be sufficient to refresh your body by allowing fresh air into your lungs. Take liquids regularly (water is best) to replenish lost body fluids which if not replenished quickly lead to a fall in alertness and diminished decision making (our bodies are more than 70% liquid).

When during a day, you decide to work is also important. Commonsense suggests that you work when you are at your freshest. Research suggests this to be in the morning, but by this point in your preparation programme, you should know which is the best time of the day for you. The nearer you get to final performance, the more you should take notice of the idea of working at the same time as you will perform in the exam room, thereby familiarising your body and mind to a similar performance routine.

Maintain a balanced routine; do not attempt both early morning and late night work!

SLEEP HELPS YOUR MEMORY TOO

We have long felt that sleep between review and recall periods is beneficial. Research now tells us that what we learned intuitively is supported by scientific research. Our memories become blurred if too much information is fed. When we are asleep our subconscious works to re-organise it in our minds. A good routine, which can be used during the Performance Stage too, is:

16th CENTURY FRENCH ESSAYIST MICHEL DE MONTAIGNE WROTE: 'WE ARE AWAKE WHILE WE ARE SLEEPING.'

1. Study during the day
2. Familiarise by reading briefly before going to bed
3. Sleep
4. Read through again in the morning.

CRAMMING

If this programme has been followed correctly, there should be no need to cram. However, if there is still a need, use it as a last resort, for those areas of the script which never seem to stick in the memory.

Cramming can only be used for short term memory – from a few minutes to a few hours. Beware of pressurising or bullying: your memory might well react against such treatment. Resist trying to force recall or demanding recall every few minutes.

WHERE TO START

It is probably best to begin with the most important parts of the Script – presumably the Division One areas – and proceed logically to Division Two, then Three, etc. Never become becalmed. If a part of the Script proves troublesome, keep going by switching focus to another area, before returning to the original section of your script. Such a strategy will maintain progress and reduce anxiety.

MEMORY SKILLS

EXPERIMENT WITH ALL THE TOOLS OF MEMORY: DISCOVER WHAT WORKS FOR YOU!

Remembering does not take place instantly or haphazardly. The efficiency of recall, the final stage of the memory system, when information is retrieved from storage, is dependent on the other parts of the system. If you have behaved sympathetically towards your memory throughout the programme, you may now be surprised just how easy it is to recall quite large sections of your Performance Script, without too much effort. So much so that you should be able to have great fun:

Keep your sessions short.

Keep your sessions light hearted

Keep your sessions exuberant

UNLOCK YOUR MEMORY BY USING ALL YOUR SENSES

ORALLY

- Recite parts of your script every day, but never insist on instant recall.
- Listen to a tape of the script spoken by you.

KINAESTHETICALLY

- Write parts of your script at speed and in a logical sequence.
- Walk in the garden or a park, reciting the Performance Script
- Perform the script with gestures and expressions

VISUALLY

- Draw diagrams or pictures.
- The brain remembers pictures more easily and for longer periods than words.

MNEMONICS – THE SMART WORD FOR MEMORY AIDS

Memory aids are invaluable. Without them recall is much much harder. Here are some you can use in your recall sessions:

DON'T BE PASSIVE:
DON'T JUST GO THROUGH THE MOTIONS BY HAVING YOUR SCRIPT OPEN IN FRONT OF YOU.
BE ACTIVE:
MEMORISE PHYSICALLY

ACTIVE RECALL

Read through a section of notes and deliberately try to commit to memory the pattern and detail of the passage. Set your notes aside and re-create the pattern and detail of the notes onto paper. Check that both are correct. If there are any errors concentrate on these.

LIVE READING OF YOUR SCRIPT

Read the Performance Script aloud, slowly, deliberately and in a relaxed frame of mind, as if you were reading a novel. Read whole sections rather than individual lines so that you obtain the full meaning. (Remember, meaning is vital to memory). Converse with yourself as to the order, pattern and organisation of the script. Say 'And now we come to the . . .', and 'Here are the five . . .'

LIVE RECALL

Recall sections of the script 'as if' to a Mastermind Chairman. Act the performance with style and humour.

LIVE TESTING

Re-use practice drafts and performance tests, either writing them out again or verbalising them, either to yourself or a friend.

LIVE PERFORMANCE
Make a tape recording of important information you want to learn. Deliberately exaggerate your reading: try to make it both funny and memorable. Play the tape in the mornings when you are dressing for the day, washing or cleaning your teeth, and at night before going to sleep.

A MUSICAL TAPE
Music is an important memory aid: it stimulate the part of the brain which controls our emotions. As you read your Script play a piece of music which is memorable to you. Better still, record yourself performing the Script against a background of incidental music, which is memorable to you.

SPEED WRITING
Challenge yourself to recall sections of your script faster and faster. Write sequences from your script, as quickly as you can. Use abbreviations to increase your speed and don't worry about your writing being legible. Scribble – you are the only person who needs to read it. It is the pace of recall that is important.

'WHAT IF' CARDS
'What If . . .' cards, containing technical or personal coping strategies can be used to reinforce your decision making.

DEFINITION LISTS
Definition list require information to be ordered and a pattern of learning established. For example:

Memorise the first definition

Memorise the second definition

Memorise the first and second together

Memorise the third definition

Repeat the first, second and third until they are correct

Memorise the fourth definition

Repeat the first, second, third and fourth until they are correct . . .

LEARNING MAPS/MIND MAPS
Learning/Mind Maps of sections of your Script allow you to see and understand the connections between pieces of knowledge.

MEMORY FLASHING
Summarise your notes into a Learning Map. Read the map through, put it aside and immediately try to recreate it. Check with the original and register any errors. Recreate the map a third time.

AD LIB TECHNIQUES
Every politician, after dinner speaker, comedian and actor knows the fear of forgetting punchlines. All develop their own techniques. Some are probably so childish that it would be embarrassing to admit them publically. Yet they enable them to perform when a performance is required.

Invent your own techniques. Here are some ideas to start you off.

Acrostics:
Inventing a sentence using the first letter of each word. For example: the musical scale: Every Good Boy Does Fine

Acronyms:
NASA: National Aeronautical Space Agency
BROM: Battles of Blenheim, Ramilles, Oudenarde and Malplaquet.

Poems, Rhymes, Lyrics:
'Mary had a little lamb'
'30 days hath September, April, June and November'
'Richard of York Gave Battle In Vain' – the letter of each word representing one of the colours of the rainbow: red, orange, yellow, green, blue, indigo, violet

'West – East' can be remembered by using the word WE, which reminds you that west is to the left.

Create Memorable Associations:
'This information reminds me of . . .'

Make Your Image Move:
Movement always adds memorability. Try moving the image of the information backwards and forwards in your mind.

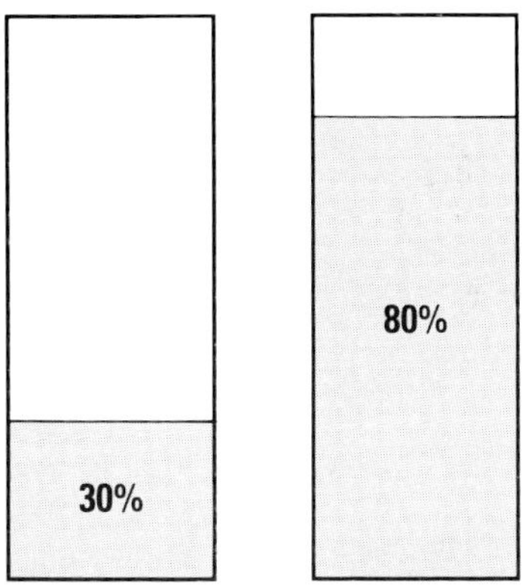

What you remember after 24 hours without a review cycle

What you remember after 6 months with a regular review

CARRY IT AND LEARN IT
Carry your script on cards wherever you go. That way you will really feel that it is a part of you. When you have a spare five minutes – in a bus queue, a traffic jam, or just waiting for someone – skim through pages to reinforce familiarisation.

OVERLOAD
Athletes deliberately overtrain so that when they compete, the final performance will feel easy. You should do the same. If you familiarise often enough it will become a part of your personal habit memory – like swimming and walking. Constant and regular familiarisation leads to substantial improvements in remembering as these bar graphs show.

WHEN YOU FORGET
When you forget something and you are trying to remember it, don't bludgeon your memory. Be sympathetic – and positive. Focus on associations with the piece of information which will help your memory and perhaps unlock the information. Another piece of 'old wisdom' which might help, is to recite the letters of the alphabet until the information is unlocked, the first letter being used to trigger recall.

STAGE 5

PERFORMANCE

INTRODUCTORY THEMES

PERFORMING IN THE EXAM ROOM IS ONLY A SMALL PART OF PERFORMANCE

The most important thing to take account of during the Performance Stage, is that performing in the exam room is only a small part of your performance. Depending on the Examination Board and the number of exams you are taking, you could be 'on stage' for between two and four weeks, during which you will perform in the examination hall maybe nine or a dozen times, sometimes three, occasionally five performances in a week. Not only is this physically demanding, but control of both yourself and your activities will be a major problem.

ORGANISING

The Performance Stage is not one single period, it is actually three periods in one – Maintenance time, during which you will maintain, and even enhance, the skills you already have, as well as making sure of your rest and recreation, Pre-Performance time, the period of time immediately before an exam, but always including the evening before, and Performance time, when you have an exam in the examination hall.

	MONDAY	TUESDAY	WEDNESDAY	THURSDAY	FRIDAY	SATURDAY	SUNDAY
a.m.	PRE EXAM	PRE EXAM		PRE	PRE EXAM		REST
lunch							
p.m. aft	MAINTENANCE	MAINTENANCE	MAINTENANCE	EXAM	MAINTENANCE	REST	REST
eve	PRE		PRE	PRE			MAYBE PRE-EXAM?

An example of a typical performance week is shown above. Three morning exams occur on Monday, Tuesday and Friday with a fourth on Thursday afternoon – a total of 12 hours inside the exam room. At least a part of three evenings are involved with Pre-Performance preparation, but four afternoons and one morning are completely free of any formal exam commitment, and the weekend is totally free. These time periods can be used either for maintenance work or rest and recreation.

CONTROL
Control is obviously crucial inside the examination hall; but it is just as crucial outside too.

PLANNING AND SCHEDULING
Plan the whole Performance Stage as soon as details become known – usually some six weeks in advance. Schedule exam performances first.

Enter: Date, time, title venue of each exam
Check: Details and whether there are clashes
Decide: How to manage the clashes

(A year or so ago some 30 candidates sitting a paper with one of the major boards 'failed' their exam because they did not spot a clash as a consequence finding themselves unable to attend one venue).

Pre-Performance periods should be scheduled next, followed by Maintenance and rest and recreational time. Recreational activities should be frequent and should complement work periods.

Be flexible – do not schedule every minute. Leave room for the unexpected, changes of plan and emergencies. Leave weekends completely free (unless Monday is a performance day). Friday and/or Saturday nights can be used as a deliberate – and glorious – reward, enjoyed all the more because you have given yourself 'permission' to enjoy yourself.

PACE
There is a temptation to live life at too fast a pace. Peak pace should be saved for performances in the exam room, the rest of your life being lived at 'a deliberately measured pace'.

THE HARDEST PART WILL BE COPING WITH THE WHOLE PERFORMANCE SITUATION. SIX OR SEVEN EXAM PERFORMANCES OVER TWO WEEKS WILL BE PHYSICALLY DRAINING

KNOWLEDGE
You may not know everything, but you should be confident that you know enough and you know how to retain it.

YOU
Like an Olympic athlete performing in the Games, a performance period which lasts a similar period of time, you have to ensure that you are in peak condition to take advantage of every opportunity, when it occurs.
Your focus should always be 'You and Your Next Performance'. Make decisions to determine the balance of work, relaxation, recreation that will enhance your next performance.

EXAMPLE: JAN

Jan took 'A' Level Business Studies in June 1989. An able student who had worked hard and conscientiously throughout the two years, she nevertheless suffered badly from exam nerves.
The evening before her last paper I telephoned her to enquire how she was getting on. 'Bored' was her reply 'I don't know what else to do.'
'Why don't you do nothing – better still, go out.' 'I couldn't do that', she replied, obviously feeling guilty, at the thought.
In the end she was persuaded to 'go out' for the evening. The next day her performance was the best of all her papers.

OUTSIDE THE EXAM ROOM

1. YOUR WORK

(a) Working Time
Work periods should never be longer than one hour at a time, and no more than three hours on any one day. On days when you have an exam, reduce maintenance to an absolute minimum – perhaps less than an hour.

(b) Don't Overwork – Take Time Off
Don't continuously pressure yourself. Your body needs time

- To absorb knowledge,
- To recover from strenuous activity
- To recover from emotional strain

You have to know when 'enough is enough', when it is better to reduce, rather than increase the volume of work. This applies particularly if you seem to have reached a major stumbling block! If this happens to you, give your body more time and space. You will be amazed and delighted by the increase in your efficiency.

Often, parents and teachers seem to expect you to work throughout the Performance Stage. Often too, a small voice inside yourself says the same! Resist this temptation. It is a symptom of stress, not control. (Revisit the Parents Section – Appendix page 71)

(c) Type of Work
The majority of your work should have been completed by the end of the Learning Stage, although some students may deliberately have left some areas of their syllabus until just before performance. Three types of work will be useful to you now:

1. Short Term Memory
2. Refreshing Memory
3. 'What If . . . Questions'

(d) Techniques
Be lighthearted and conversational with yourself. You are only trying to 'top up knowledge.'

Say – 'What is Elasticity of Demand?

Say – 'Hey there, tell me what consumption is?

Say – 'There are 4 types of ratios analysing final accounts – can you tell me what they are?'

Use the 'What If' technique:

Say – 'What if they want to know about the Repeal of the Corn Laws – can you tell me about that?

2. YOUR RECREATION AND RELAXATION

Relaxation and recreation are vital parts of your performance preparation. Any number of activities can be used:

walking the dog,
playing tennis,
lounging with friends,
running across the country,
watching TV,
swimming,
going for a drive,
being with a special person

The need for relaxation and recreation must be acknowledged and time made available. This is especially so late in the day. Before going to bed try listening to some soothing music, or unwinding physically by using a relaxation technique. Relaxation is so important, it might be worthwhile revisiting the Planning Stage, (page 48).

3. YOUR FRIENDS

Your friends are a part of your preparation (if not your performance), whether you want them to be or not! Deliberately bring them within your plan of preparation.

Some friends will always be a great help, particularly in times of stress and anxiety (the Performance Stage is likely to be just such a time). Others will be less helpful. Include, as often as you think correct, those people who will help you – be the help academic or recreational. Exclude, those people who spend hours boring you with their troubles – 'they can't sleep, are becoming mad with worry, are on tranquillisers' – who – thereby transfer their stress to you.

4. YOUR CLOSE RELATIONSHIPS

Close relationships can be of great help during this particular period, but be aware that they may also cause problems. When one person is under pressure, disagreements over the most minor things are likely.

It might be best to talk this through in advance with your friend(s), with parents and other close relatives. While they may need to make allowances for you, you may need to make allowances for them!

5. YOUR PHYSICAL ACTIVITIES

Exam performances are physically punishing. They exert considerable pressure on your body. When your brain is working to the extent that (we anticipate) it will be during the Performance Stage, the nerve cells burn energy at an increased rate. Stress, in the form of nervous energy, also burns energy faster than usual.

Recognise and acknowledge this. Deliberately plan; make a decision that you will replace the supply of energy your body needs throughout the Performance Stage.

Eat regularly and sensibly
Exams are not a good time to diet! Fruit and salads are good, but high intake of sugar and caffeine, both of which increase arousal, should be avoided, unless they are for a specific and short term purpose.
If you feel hungry you should eat. This will reduce the stress you are experiencing. If you don't feel like food, you should still eat. Trying something different may help.

Drink regularly and sensibly
Caffeine (coffee and tea) which encourages adrenaline production should be avoided. Herb teas, fruit juices, mineral or ordinary tap water are better. Milk, which contains naturally occurring morphine-like substances is calming.

Sleep regularly
For as long as you are able. Sleep is not only calming, it allows your sub conscious to work for you too.

Exercise regularly and sensibly. Live life at a measured controlled pace.

EXAMPLES OF STUDENTS' ACTIVITIES IN THE PERFORMANCE STAGE
These examples are taken from answers to the Physical Needs Questionnaire, Planning Stage, page 56).

Students took part in some form of physical activity 3/4 times a week, the most popular activities being tennis and swimming. Other relaxation methods that were used were listening to music, watching TV and going out with friends. The main reasons given by students for their relaxation were: – need of a physical break, allow mind to recover, release of tension, a change of focus, and a break from the boredom of constant revision.

EATING HABITS
More than half the students found that their eating habits changed during the revision and exam period.

'I eat more because when I have a break I go downstairs and munch.'
'I eat 3 very well balanced meals a day.'
'I tend to eat less than normal especially immediately before an exam, but I do eat more carbohydrates the day before.'
'I cat more regularly.'
'I eat more – 3 main meals plus snacks in between.'
'I am much more conscientious, and make sure I eat decent meals at proper times. I wouldn't normally do this.'

SLEEPING HABITS
On the whole, the students were evenly split about their sleeping habits during the exam period. Half found that they did not sleep well and gave 'worry' about the forthcoming exam as the main reason. Whilst others found that they were more 'tired' and therefore required more sleep.
The number of hours slept on average . . . 8-9 hours.

Without exception every student said that this was MORE than they normally have!.

The following are examples of what students said when asked if there was any more information that they felt was important in relation to their physical needs during the exam period.

'I think it would be rewarding to keep yourself fit because when you feel good with yourself you seem to achieve more. Also you wouldn't get depressed because you were looking bad.'

'Don't sit inside all day, go outside for walks etc.'

'I learnt that any method of relaxation was very important. I made sure that I did some walking and I told myself not to worry about this being a waste of time. It wasn't and it worked.'

'I found that being able to revise with a group or one or two people made the task much easier. We were all in the same position. If you became nervous about an exam, friends were always there to help build up your confidence. Communication is essential, it doesn't seem like such hard work either.'

'Yoga or other relaxation methods help ease muscle and mental fatigue.'

'Mentally controlling nerves and panic seems more important to me. It is also important that family, friends and especially parents understand what we need. We're not really normal during this time.'

'Encouragement to go occasionally from parents.'

6. YOUR OWN PERFORMANCE ROUTINE

Routines increase control, security and confidence. Use a sheet of paper to decide the routine that feels best for you, encompassing all the types of activity discussed above. Build the routine into your performance programme by making it a habit.

CONTROLLING YOUR INTERNAL FEELINGS

The mix of feelings you experience during the Performance Stage are inevitably difficult to control.

So much is happening:
- You are at last actually performing in the exam room.
- During other work periods maintain your readiness to perform.
- Pre-performance routines require your attention.
- There may be hours, sometimes days seemingly spare between exams.

So much seems to hang on a very short period of time:
- The exams probably loom very large.
- You are well aware that your parents are hoping you will do well.
- Your friends are feeling exactly the same.
- You have other friends who keep asking you out!

Everything may appear to be in conflict!

YOUR MENTAL SKILLS

Enjoyment of the Performance Stage is often impaired by your feelings and emotions, unless your mental skills are used to retain and recover control. First recognise how you are feeling, and then acknowledge what your emotions are.

Constant evaluation is necessary.

YOU

internal evaluation

Which skills can be regarded as being – good	Which skills can be regarded as being – not so good
Eg: Relaxation Anxiety Stress Confidence	eg: Concentration Distractions Arousal

Having categorised your feelings, give yourself a pat on the back over those which are OK. Then decide what you will do about the others. Those that are outside your control, acknowledge – but stop worrying about them because you can do nothing about them! Re-focus on those you can do something about – prioritise them, make decisions and plan how they can be improved.

MORALE
Morale is an element of performance that is rarely constant; it is either rising or falling. High morale is NOT automatic. To be maintained (or retrieved) requires a considerable amount of work. Positive self talk is vital.

YOUR MOTIVATION – AND BOREDOM
The programme has been running for the best part of four months. Boredom at this stage is very likely. Tell yourself that the exams are nearly over now. Promise to reward yourself as soon as the exams are over. Positive Self Talk – and remember the example of Jan (page 129).

PHYSICAL TIREDNESS
Physical tiredness will accumulate as the stage proceeds. It should not be dismissed lightly.

Adopt a good personal routine – regular eating, as much sleep as the body requires, and the right mix of performance, work, relaxation, exercise and recreation.

DISTRACTIONS
These may be a part of boredom or they may be a compelling part of 'the rest of your life' – which you long to re-join.
Concentration is important: 'Stay in the Present and ask constantly: 'What is the next thing to do'.

ANXIETY
Anxiety is a part of performances. You can control it by adopting the right techniques (see Planning Stage page 45)

SELF DOUBT
Self Doubt, either past, present or future, is also a part of performance. Positive self talk and the discipline to 'stay in the present' are the required skills (see Planning Stage page 33).

POST MORTEMS

Post mortems are a feature of exam performances everyone will recognise. Once an exam is ended, not only will you think about your own performance, other people will talk to you about theirs. They say: 'Which questions did you do? . . . Didn't you do Question A, that was a cinch!' . . . 'Question 2 was horrid, you didn't do that, did you? . . . and so on.

Usually such conversations are 'a lot of irrelevant hot air.' Everyone is so close to the actual performance that whatever is said is highly subjective and very emotional. Very few people speak the truth; post mortems like this are best avoided.

YOUR OWN POST EXAM ROUTINE
Your own Post Exam Routine is quite different. Your past performances have to be evaluated. This should be an essential part of your performance routine, which will help control and improve your future performances. Be serious about it. Use pen and paper to evaluate every aspect of your performance (technical and mental) paying greater attention to your personal routines (which are transferable to the next performance) than to the technical aspects (which, being specific, are not).

Retain those parts of your routine which work. Discard those parts which do not.

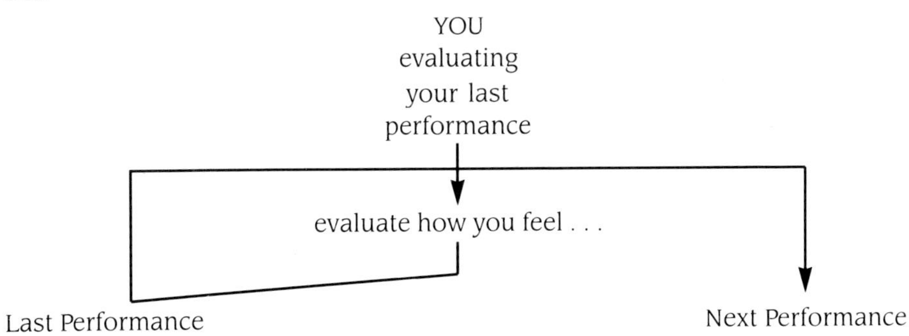

These are the kind of questions to ask:

When, before the exam, did I last read the Performance Script? Was this the right time? Did I read it sufficiently slowly?
When did I have feelings of anxiety before the exam?
What did I do about it? How well did I control my feelings?
Did my 'confidence checklist' work for me?
Which parts of my Pre-Performance Routine worked well/badly

If you analyse correctly and evaluate realistically, your future performances will be enhanced. However, it is important to remember that quite often students misjudge their performances. When they think they have done badly, they have actually done quite well. Everything is relative – if the paper seemed difficult to you, undoubtedly it will have appeared so to other students. As a result, the pass and grading marks will be lower.

No matter how you performed previously, the most important performance is always 'the next one'. Those performances which are in the past – even the recent past – are absolutely outside your control and therefore irrelevant to your planning.

Those in front of you are well and truly under your control. Focus on these. Speak positively to yourself. Have confidence that the knowledge is already within you, that it will be there when you require it, and that recall is very probable.

Believe – and don't pressure yourself!

DEPROGRAMME AFTER AN EXAM

Immediately after any exam try to have a period of complete relaxation. Your mind and body are very like a computer; you have a need to 'deprogramme' before you begin to put in new information.
Choose an activity you know will relax you and will act as a simple distraction – eat, watch TV, go for a walk, sleep, rest, read, chat. Do this, even if you have another exam the same day. Perhaps, particularly if you have an exam the same day!

PRE PERFORMANCE ROUTINES

GOOD PERFORMANCES BEGIN WELL IN ADVANCE OF THEIR COMMENCEMENT

A FEW DAYS BEFORE

Do a Health Check:
If you suffer from hay fever or some other persistent medical problem, seek help from your GP.

Be careful of using painkillers (eg: for painful periods); they can cause drowsiness.

Do An Equipment Check:
Check all the equipment you will need.

- Spare pens, cartridges, ink, pencils
- Calculators, rulers, protractors, erasers
- Anything else (lucky charms, cards, etc) you have made a part of your performance equipment.

If these are not checked early, they can cause panic the night before – when it might be too late to do anything about them!

THE EVENING BEFORE

Pre Performance always begins the evening before, whether your exam is in the morning or the afternoon.

MENTAL REHEARSAL:
Spend no more than 40/60 minutes (Refer to Planning Stage page 44)
a) Prepare a tight Performance Plan. Begin when you walk into the exam room and proceed stage by stage – attune, read the paper, select, plan, answer the questions.
b) Prepare 5/6 topics in outline, together with concept definitions and your own 'What If . . .' solutions.

THEN RELAX
Do something you enjoy doing – watch a movie, or a video, read a book, listen to music . . . or go out!

BUDGET YOUR TIME:
A Good Plan = A Good Performance
For a 3 hour paper your budget might be:

Planning Time	=	15 minutes
Work Time	=	150 minutes
Checking Time	=	10 minutes
Spare Time	=	5 minutes

This budget, which is generous on planning and spare time, suggests 30 minutes per question if five have to be answered, 37 minutes if only four. Use this budget with care and flexibility, but beware of curtailing planning time.

LAST THING AT NIGHT
To increase memorisation and recall, read the relevant parts of your Performance Script(s) immediately before going to sleep.

SLEEP
Allow your subconscious to work for you. Your brain works during the night to make sense of the information received during the day. Sleep is a major influence on your memory's storage system.

MORNINGS FOR A MORNING EXAM

WAKE UP:
Straightaway develop a positive attitude. Speak positively to yourself: 'I feel great this morning'.
Re-read the Performance Script, slowly and deliberately, or listen to your audio tape while you are dressing, washing, making up.

MEMORY:
DO NOT attempt to test your memory by practising recall. Deliberately relax and reassure yourself that you will remember when you have to! Tell yourself that this is so.

CONFIDENCE CHECKLIST:
Run through your confidence checklist.

BREAKFAST:
You should eat – that is for sure!
Carbohydrates are often suggested, but in reality it does not matter too much what you eat – so long as you do.
Missing breakfast could mean that your body goes for as long as 15 hours without the food it needs to replenish energy. That is a very long time.

MENTAL REHEARSAL:
You may not feel this is necessary, or you might run through five major sections of your script, and some 'What If . . .' solutions. Memorise any short term memory items. (Refer to Planning Stage, page 44).

DEPARTURE
Leave for your performance at the right time for you.

MORNINGS FOR AN AFTERNOON EXAM
Up to breakfast time, nothing is different. After breakfast there will be more time to control. Maybe:

MORNING WORK PERIOD:
With more time, your mental rehearsal can be more thorough. Perhaps organise a short, lighthearted test, or work at pace through a Performance Test or two.

RELAXATION:
Whatever suits you – even preparing for another exam! If you really have practised enough replace your work session with relaxation.

DEPARTURE:
Leave for your performance at the right time for you.

PRE PERFORMANCE ROUTINE AT THE EXAM CENTRE
TIME OF ARRIVAL:
This should be sufficient to accomplish everything calmly and without a rush. Not everyone's needs are the same: calculate the amount of time you need and make it a part of your routine.

ATTUNE:
As soon as you arrive . . . begin attuning to the performance environment and the people who are a part of it. This might include talking with friends, or just becoming used to the idea of performance. If you do talk with friends, make sure that this works for you and not against you.

PHYSICAL NEEDS:
Visit the toilet
Have a drink of water
Clean you glasses (if you wear them)

SWITCH ON:
'Switch on' always occurs, whether you are aware of it or not. Therefore bring it under your control; make it a part of your performance. Begin to focus on how this will be done.

AROUSAL:
Everyone's arousal level is different – some people need arousal increasing, others decreasing. Adopt the correct strategy for you. (Planning Stage – page 48).

MENTAL REHEARSAL:
Practise mentally 5 major concepts. (Planning Stage – page 44)

MEMORY:
Think positively; believe and trust your memory.
If however there are some parts of your Performance Script which you find particularly difficult – graphs, quotes, dates, formulae, ratios, (everyone will have their own memory blocks) – memorise the information immediately before

entering the exam room. Inside, write them onto rough paper as soon as you are able. Once you have read the paper and found you need them – smile! And, if they are not required, crumple the paper – and smile even more. After all you have done your preparation well. Reward yourself – and enjoy the feeling.

A FINAL REMINDER:
All this takes time – have you left enough?
And.
If your arrival at the exam centre is delayed for some reason, and your ideal routine cannot be effected, have you a 'Plan B'?
Plan B should include the absolute essentials – what you feel you must do, come what may, the remainder being relegated as inessentials.

THE FINAL PERFORMANCE: INSIDE THE EXAM ROOM

THE IDEA OF A GOOD PERFORMANCE

A good performance occurs when the right skills are used, in the right way, at the right time, so that the desired objective is achieved.

Performing is all about:

- Allowing yourself to use the skills you already have.
- Releasing your knowledge onto paper to impress the examiner.
- Integrating all your skills in a final performance.

STRATEGIES FOR EXAM PERFORMANCE

THE BEST PERFORMERS ARE NOT NECESSARILY THE MOST TALENTED. THEY RE THE PEOPLE WHO COPE BEST WITH PERFORMANCE SITUATIONS; WHO GIVE THEMSELVES PERMISSION TO USE THEIR KNOWLEDGE, WHO ALLOW THEIR ABILITIES TO PERFORM. WHO DO NOT TRY TO SABOTAGE THEIR PERFORMANCE!

No matter how hard you have worked, or how thoroughly you have prepared, your exam success now depends entirely on how well you control your performance in the examination hall. This starts when you decide your strategy. Although it may be adjusted once you are in the exam room and have read the paper, it should be decided outside the exam room a day or two before.

Strategies are personal to a student and specific to a performance. The overall plan a student decides to use to reach the goals they have set is determined by the student's perception of their ability, relative to their perception of the nature and difficulty of the exam paper.

Three basic choices are available – accumulation, optimisation and maximisation – although all three can be qualified by student once the paper has been read.

1. Accumulation
This strategy should be used by students who are either less sure of their technical ability, or unsure whether they can fully complete a paper within the time limits.

It works best in quantitative, data response or case study papers which have a large number of structured questions, each of which require a significant proportion of reading time.

Students should not worry if they cannot complete the whole paper, or whole questions, so long as they accumulate as many marks as they can, as they proceed through their performance. Provided that the methods of work and a substantial part of the calculation is correct, questions may be left unfinished (or incorrect in their final answer).

2. Optimisation
Every car owner will appreciate the difference between optimum and maximum performance. A car's optimal performance – a speed of 50-55 mph, which gives maximum consumption of petrol and minimum wear and tear to the engine – is quite different to its maximum speed and acceleration, both of which are achieved at considerable extra cost.

Optimal strategies aim to produce the most consistent and efficient results throughout the duration of a performance.

Using the strategy in an essay paper requires the student to write four 'fair to middling' essays rather than 'busting a gut' to write one essay which achieves 80%, while the other three, perhaps through lack of time, lack of energy or both, are relatively poor.

In a quantitative paper it means that students can be satisfied with answers in which the techniques and methods are correct, even if the final answer is either incorrect or unfinished. Optimal strategies are good because they help control time, they focus on effective and consistent performance and they allow commonsense to triumph over pride!

3. Maximisation
Maximal performances aim to produce the highest possible marks irrespective of cost measured by tiredness, poor time control and too narrow a focus! They are used best by highly capable and very confident students in quantitative, multiple choice, or data response papers in which a very high score is a feasible target.

USING STRATEGIES: STAY IN THE PRESENT
Although strategies are planned in advance of performance, the real skill of using them is understanding whether or not they are working, and if not, whether they can be changed, and when! Try never to hold 'hard and fast' expectations about either the nature of the paper, or the choice of questions. Pre-conceived notions are dangerous, because they move you into the future. If you do this, you may not be able to cope and will contribute to sabotaging your own performance.

Stay in the present. Be prepared to 'wait and see', to make sure your analysis of difficulty is correct, so that decisions can be made on 'what is' rather than on 'what you thought might be.'

CONTROLLING YOUR EXAM PERFORMANCE IN THE EXAM ROOM

(Although this section addresses particular situations likely to be found in the actual examination room, some of the techniques may be used at other times during the Performance Stage)

PERSONAL CONTROL IS ACHIEVED THROUGH TACTICS AND SKILL

The following performance elements need controlling:

The Start of the Exam
Selection of Questions
Planning Your Answers
Working Your Answers
Controlling Your Pace
Controlling Your Time
Controlling Your Feelings and maybe
Controlling Emergencies = damage limitation.

Tactics, the behaviours required for a successful outcome, to achieve precise performance goals and to allow you to respond to changes in circumstances, enable you to control your overall performance.

THE START OF THE EXAM

One would like to think that students will have perfected their 'start of an exam' behaviour by practising their routine from the beginning of the Familiarisation Stage. Here is a sequence to use in actual performance:

ATTUNE:
The period of time from your entering the room to the invigilator starting the exam can be used to attune to the atmosphere and ambience of the exam room.

Allow yourself to 'feel' the room – its temperature, light, smells, and noise (or lack of it compared to other environments in which you have studied) together with the arrangement of desks and the proximity of people, particularly those likely to prove a distraction.

RELAX:
Deliberately relax your whole body, particularly neck, shoulders and upper back, using a deep breathing technique.

Stress, anxiety and pressure, all of which make students tense, are always present at the beginning of exams. When you are tense, your whole body tightens, and your focus narrows, reducing the effectiveness of your skills and decision making.

EXAMPLE

Research carried out by the AEB shows that exam takers fall into two categories, planners and rushers. The planners, who take time to read the whole paper and select their questions with care, perform better. Rushers make serious errors in their anxiety to get on.

One who received only two out of a possible twenty four marks for a chosen question, admitted to the researchers that it wasn't the question he had meant to do, but as he had started it he carried on!

George Turnbull (Associated Examination Board)

Relaxation is an important skill many times during performance, but at the start of an exam, it is crucial. Avoid strait jacketing yourself. Make time for relaxation.

Switch On:
Focus on having a positive attitude.
Speak – positively to yourself.
Think – only positive thoughts.
Use – your performance routine.

Write your name and number on answer sheets. Listen carefully to the invigilator's instructions.

2: SELECTION
Selecting the right questions is one of the most important parts of performance strategy. Adopt the filtering model:

THE SELECTION FILTER

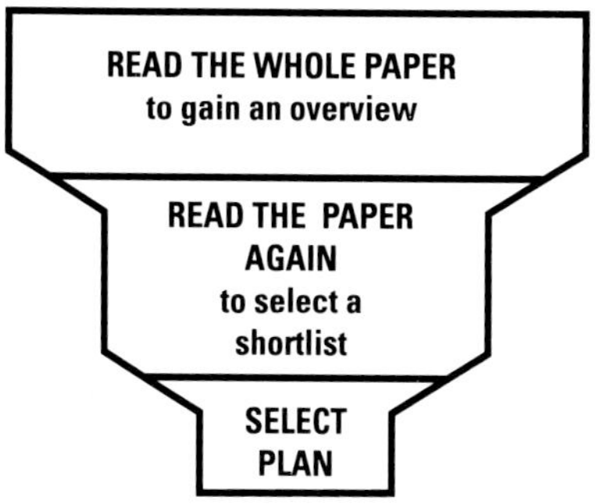

WHY?
SOME FIVE YEARS AGO A STUDENT WHO WAS NOT PARTICULARLY CONFIDENT ABOUT HER PAPER TOOK BUSINESS STUDIES A LEVEL. DURING A MEETING IMMEDIATELY BEFORE THE EXAM SHE ASKED TO HAVE HER MEMORY REFRESHED ON CAPITAL INVESTMENT APPRAISAL.
AN IDENTICAL QUESTION TO THE ONE WE HAD DISCUSSED APPEARED ON HER PAPER.
GREETING HER AFTERWARDS I SAID: 'YOU MUST HAVE BEEN PLEASED WITH THE DCF QUESTION?
SHE REPLIED: 'WHAT DCF QUESTION?
PUZZLED, I BEGAN TO EXPLAIN. THEN I TUMBLED TO THE TRUTH. THE DCF QUESTION HAD BEEN THE LAST QUESTION – GINA HAD NOT TURNED OVER THE LAST PAGE AND THEREFORE HAD NOT SEEN IT!

As soon as you are able:
Read the whole paper quickly – scan to obtain a 'feel'.
– to see your opportunities.
Make sure you read to the end!

Re-read the paper again to pre-select questions:
Read slowly
Again, read to the end
Avoid making too quick a decision.
Avoid focusing on questions that appeal to you
Analyse (Ask questions: what concept is involved in the question?)

Re-read your shortlisted questions:
Analyse, to determine major concepts
Highlight key phrases
Doodle: Use margin and rough paper
Check that you understand both types of message – technical and instructional.
Do not disregard questions which appear too simple, but double check their messages.
Select those questions you can do best, or most easily.
Select at this stage, three out of four, or four out of five.

3. PLANNING
Begin planning answers immediately. Use this time as an extra part of attunement. Mistakes often occur at the beginning of a performance; this way they occur under your control.

THE STORY OF THE BRICKLAYER
Recently, I had a wall built in my garden. The first bricklayer I employed looked at the plans and the site – and very quickly began laying bricks. Too quickly as it turned out; his line was all wrong! Four courses later he was dismissed!

A second bricklayer was employed. He spent a whole morning – BEFORE A BRICK WAS LAID – looking at the plan, the site, and playing around with the lines of bricks on the ground to see which line looked right.

NEVER ATTEMPT TO PERFORM WITHOUT PLANNING: DON'T RUSH: MAKE SURE YOU LAY A SOLID FOUNDATION BEFORE YOU PROCEED!

He stayed on the job until completion. His technical skills may have been no better than the first workman, but his range of skills was wider. He had the patience and control to integrate all his skills, into a single performance at the right pace.

WHEN PLANNING, USE ROUGH PAPER, it is a vital aid
Plan at least two, perhaps three questions at the beginning of the exam BEFORE you write any answers for the examiner.
Decide: where to start and then how the answer will proceed.

USE THE INVERTED PYRAMID (See familiarisation, page 109)

USE 'THE BUTTERFLY NET'
Everyone's mind works differently and sometimes the patterns are very idiosyncratic – perhaps particularly during exam performances! Thoughts enter the mind from many different directions, often seemingly at random.
If these patterns are acknowledged, they can be made to work for you rather than against you. All that is needed is a control mechanism within which to catch and organise these elusive thoughts.

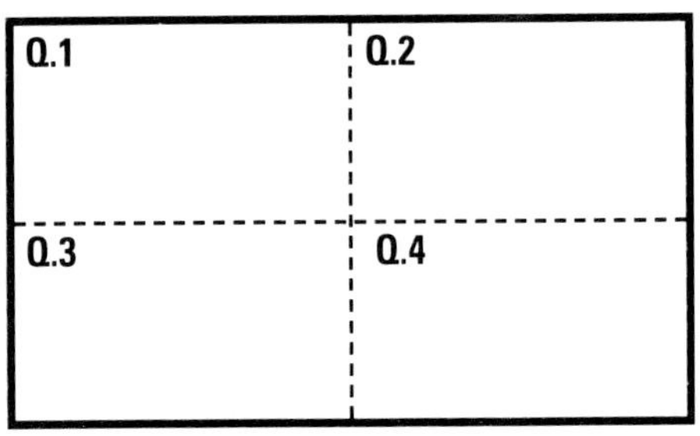

A piece of rough paper subdivided into segments can be your 'butterfly net'. Whenever a thought crosses your mind it can be caught and entered in the right segment. Later it can be re-organised into a logical pattern and used to answer the question.

The 'Butterfly Net' takes pressure off your memory. It also increased your control, and by doing so, increases your self confidence too.

4. WORK
CONTROL THE ORDER
The order in which questions are answered is a part of your control system. Answer first the questions you feel happiest about, or can do the fastest. If you re-order the sequence of questions, begin each on a new sheet of paper. Controlling the order in which questions are answered will boost your confidence, give you a real sense of progress and enable you to have a better control of time.

CONTROL THE SEQUENCE
ALWAYS – think first and write second. DO NOT try to do these two things together.

5. PACE
The pace at which a person works is a major factor influencing success. If the pace is too quick, there is a tendency to make mistakes: too slow and time runs out before the performance is complete.

Students who think that once an exam has started they should work 'flat out' are in error. Pace should be varied to complement the tasks being performed, the correct speed being chosen from 'a three speed gearing system':

1. Relaxing Speed: almost zero. Used to take a break.
2. Thinking Speed: deliberately slow. Used to think through solutions, to plan and organise answers.
3. Working Speed: almost a sprint. Used to write your answer down as quickly as possible.

PACE CONTROL DURING A 3 HOUR / 4 QUESTION EXAM

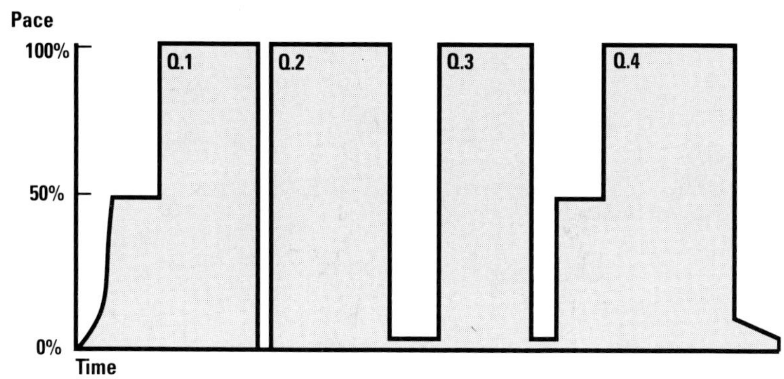

6. TIME
Time, which during an exam is in short supply, is a major source of pressure and stress, particularly if your performance does not go according to plan. Time is therefore a major focus.

SEEING TIME
Although time proceeds at a standard speed, everyone has the power to increase or decrease their perceptions of its speed.
If time appears to be running away from you, slow your perception down by:
Deliberately slowing the pace of your thoughts, slowing your self talk. 'Doodling' your thoughts onto paper. Reassure yourself that you do have x minutes left – and that that is enough to do what you have to do.
Visualise time in such a way that it slows down.
If you see time coming towards you, its appearance is faster than if you visualise it stretching into the distance (Refer to Familiarisation page 119).

SCHEDULING TIME
An important part of Pre-Performance strategy concerns setting time budgets; they will be your control systems during perfomrance. Time goals should be

decided and a written plan made, itemising each segment of performance, as well as start and finish times for each question.

An initial budget my use 'equal time for each question.' However, once the paper has been read, a more flexible plan based on the allocation of marks for each question might be used, no greater time being spent on a question than the number of marks alloted to it.

BUILD A TIME BANK
A 'time bank' is a good tool to use to achieve your time goals. At the start of a performance, time will have been allocated according to plan and 'time in the bank' will be zero. One performance goal should be to build a positive stock of 'time in the bank' by completing question 1, then 2, then 3, ahead of schedule. If, by the halfway stage, you have achieved a positive stock of time, your pace can be slowed, or your allocation of time can be adjusted. If your stock is negative, the fact that you have set a time goal can still be used as an incentive to control time in the next segment of performance. Having a 'time bank' ensures that time goals are at the forefront of your performance routine.

TIME TACTICS; MAKING DECISIONS ABOUT TIME
1. Attitude
Have a positive and disciplined attitude towards control of time. Deliberately intend time control to be important. Try to stick to your plan – use your watch every ten minutes – but be flexible if this is the correct tactic.

2. Checkpoints
Natural checkpoints occur at the end of each question. Major checkpoints should be built in – at the halfway stage and 40 minutes from the end.

3. Reschedule
At the halfway stage you may need to change the schedule. Rescheduling might also be a useful change of focus which allows you a moment's relaxation.

4. Over-running
As a general rule time discipline should be ruthless. But if the temptation to over-run occurs make better decisions by reference to:
   a) Principle of Comparative Margins
      Extra time spent on a question is only worthwhile if the extra time yields a greater number of marks than if a new question had been attempted. In almost all cases it is better to attempt a new question.
      If extra time is spent on the present question the most one can expect is 3 or 4 extra marks. If a new question is attempted the minimum should be 8 or 9. Gymnasts recognise that it is much easier to move from 5.1 to 5.2 than from 5.9 to 6.0. Recognise this too.

b) Sufficiency
Recognise that on any exam paper there are marks that are superfluous to your purpose.
To gain a Grade A (Grade 7 in IB) requires 70-75% depending on the norm. At least 25% of the marks are superfluous. No one ever knows whether you gain 80%, 90% or even 100%.

An important part of your personal control system is to recognise that you can make some marks irrelevant to your strategy – they can be literally 'thrown away'. For instance, in some numerical questions, it is more important to show the examiner the right way to solve the problem than to achieve precisely the right answer. It is better to move from this question to the next making a note that IF there is spare time at the end it might be possible to return to it then.

The same is true of papers which contain a large number of individual questions or structured questions broken into segments. (eg: Business Studies Paper 1). It is possible to gain a high grade if two and a half questions are done really well, and the fourth only tolerably so. An exam strategy need not aim to finish all four questions.

5. Running out of time:
No matter the excellence of the budget, students often begin to run out of time. At this point a coping strategy is necessary. A note form answer will gain only a small number of marks, It is better to start the last question as if intending to finish, write a part of the answer and then finish off in note form. In maths an outline of how to solve the problem might be given, quoting formulae and stating where and how you could quote missing values.'

7. FEELINGS
At the beginning of a performance, no matter the feelings of excitement and nervousness you may have, it is to be hoped that you will be both relaxed and confident. Too often however, students feel either under or over aroused, sometimes amounting almost to panic.
If you are under aroused, increase arousal by:

- Talking to yourself
- 'Take a grip on yourself': sit up straight, tense the muscles of your shoulders, chest and stomach. Act being alert!
- Make all your movements positive and urgent.

If you are over-aroused, relax by:

- STOPPING WORK
- Recognise and acknowledge the symptoms of over-arousal
- Analyse why this situation has occurred; what are the reasons?
- Relax your body – use slow, deep breathing techniques.
  – talk yourself down, speaking deliberately, calmly, slowly.
  – close your eyes and imagine a soft, quiet, peaceful scene for a moment or two.
- Do something positive about the cause of your over-arousal.
  OR

- Refocus onto the next thing to be done.

If you start to lose concentration, get it back by:

- Recognising the symptoms – your external focus becomes
  multiple
  blurred
  hectic

your internal focus becomes
  multiple
  blurred
  hectic

- Acknowledge the causes of your loss of concentration: the internal/external distractions.
- Control by – positive self talk to refocus correctly
  – positive self talk to redirect your energy

Remember to reward yourself with a smile!

If you begin to feel pressure or stress, control by:

- STOPPING WORK
- Take a short break. Allow your mind and body to wander, to go 'walkabout'. Daydream in fact.

Again – reward yourself with a smile, because you know what you are doing and why!

If you become physically tired, refresh yourself by:
You may feel mentally tired before you feel physically so. Nevertheless, the feeling has to be controlled.

- Take a brief rest period.
- Have 40 winks, a cat nap.
- Daydream, take a holiday somewhere in your mind.
- When this is over, go back to work having first talked determinedly to yourself.

AND, MAINTAIN YOUR CONFIDENCE AND MORALE.
KEEP ENCOURAGING YOURSELF.
TICK OFF QUESTIONS WHEN YOU FINISH THEM.
CONGRATULATE YOURSELF.
'WELL DONE, IT'S GOING WELL, NOW FOR THE NEXT . . .

If you doubt your memory, support it.

- Don't doubt: support it and be sympathetic.
- As soon as you are able in the exam room, jot down on rough paper the items you might forget during the exam.
- Continue to use 'rough paper' as a memory bank, jotting down concepts, ideas, and thoughts when they occur.

When this book was being written, an Open University Programme on BBC-1 signed off, what it called its revision programme, with the words
'All that is left now is for us to wish you good luck in your examinations!'

You should know better than this now.
You should know that:

LUCK HAS NOTHING TO DO WITH IT!
YOU MAKE YOUR OWN LUCK,
BY GOOD PREPARATION

ENJOY YOUR PERFORMANCE

APPENDIX

1. STUDY SKILLS

NOTEMAKING TECHNIQUES

There are as many different types of notes, as there are reasons for making them, ranging from the odd jotting made during lectures, to comprehensive summaries, spray diagrams, mind maps and skeleton outlines. Notemaking is a major activity within any programme of study, the exact type chosen being determined by the purpose to which they will be put. Quite correctly many students spend a great deal of their time making and remaking notes.

Notes are an important part of exam preparation too. In the Organisation Stage, when your notes are being organised into a performance script, linear notes, which use the classical skeleton outline are probably best. During the Familiarisation Stage tree diagrams, sequencing and graphic organisers are useful because they present information visually and in a tightly organised way which helps the memory. Learning Maps and Mind Maps, which link pieces of knowledge together within an overall pattern and are quick and enjoyable to use, are especially useful during the Learning and Performance Stages.

ALTERNATIVE LAYOUTS
No notemaking layout can ever be described as 'best on all occasions.' All have their strengths and weaknesses and will appeal to different people, for different reasons and uses, at different stages of preparation.

The Classical layout is excellent when writing detailed notes, but there are a multitude of different techniques which are fun to use.

I.
    A.
    B.
    C.
        1.
        2.
        3.

II. A.
    B.
        1.
        2.
            a.
            b.
            c.

TREE DIAGRAM

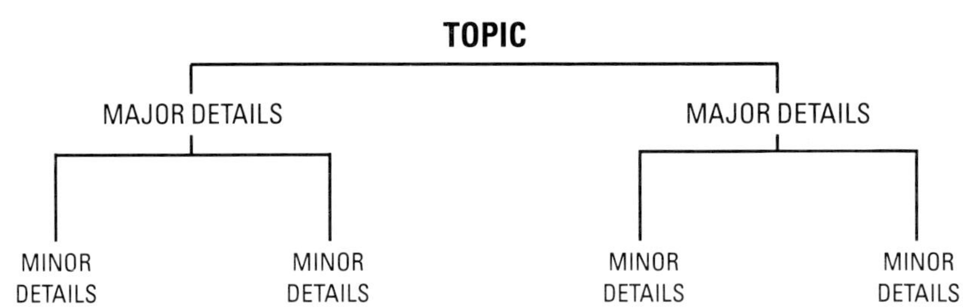

MAPPING

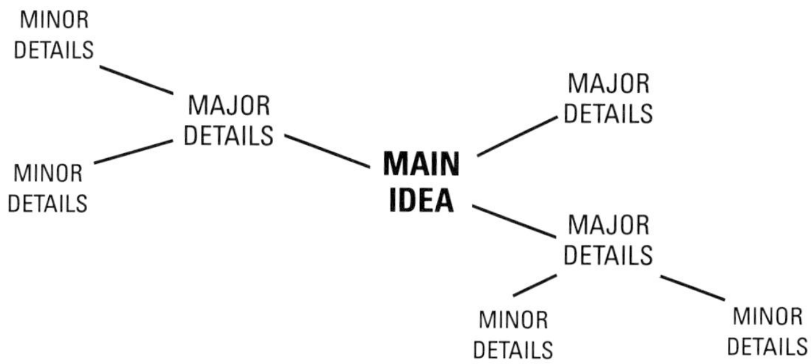

MAPPING

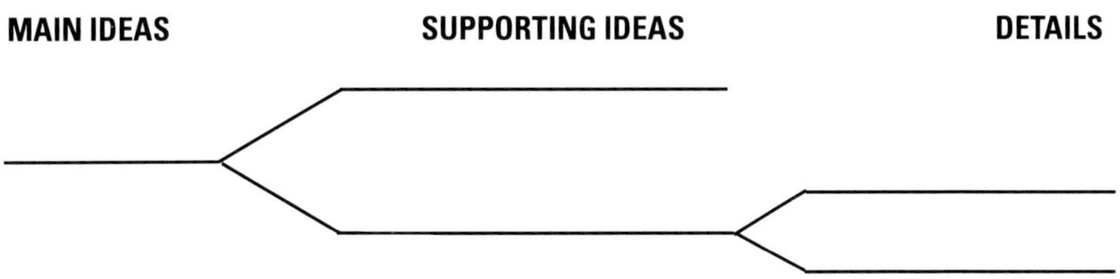

WRITING DRAFT/SKELETON ANSWERS

Answers written in outline or noteform are known as draft or skeleton answers. Drafts are especially useful during the Familiarisation Stage because they increase:

- Control of knowledge
- Control of the use of knowledge
- Control of selection
- Control of planning and organisation
- Speed of thought, speed or writing.

The bare bones of an answer, organised in the right pattern can be quickly and clearly written, to answer the question. The outline, being brief and to the point, can then be used when visualising or mentally rehearsing notes before performance.

Prior to writing – think and organise
1. THINKING – WHAT DOES THE QUESTION REQUIRE FROM ME?
Ask the right questions

Of the Question.
eg: What kind of question is it?
Definitive, Analytical, Open-ended, etc?
What instructional words are used?

Of the Knowledge.
eg: What kind of question is being asked?
What are the Key Concepts?
What are the Key Factors?
What support is required? Examples?

2. ORGANISATION – WHAT IS THE PATTERN OF THE ANSWER?
Introduction – Definition: what?
Explanation: what?
Mainstream – How will it be subdivided?
What signposts are required?
Conclusion – How to end?

WRITING THE DRAFT

LENGTH
One side of paper is best; certainly not longer than $1\frac{1}{2}$ sides.

VISUAL ORGANISATION
Should be a major concern, it is a major aid to memory.

STANDARD FORMAT
Maintain a standard format/routine when writing drafts so that your mind and eye become familiar with your work processes.

SUBHEADINGS
Should be titles, signposts – set on the left of the page.

KEY WORDS
Should be at the beginning of line.

DETAIL
Should be organised under numbered points. Dashes and commas being used, if information is more than one piece. If information runs for more than one line, indent the beginning to emphasise the signpost word.

TYPES OF EXAM QUESTIONS

Responding to questions is one of the key skills of examination performances. A guide to the main types of questions currently used by examiners is given below.

1. MECHANICAL QUESTIONS
Mechanical questions are often used in science subjects and the quantitative areas of social science subjects. A route map is the best technique to use. Once the correct starting point has been established, a step by step route map can be determined. Once understood, it can be learnt and practised before performance.

2. SHORT STRUCTURED QUESTIONS
A wide range of subjects use structured questions. They appear in quantitative, case study, data response and essay papers.

In an essay paper structuring make the question easier because some of the planning has been done for you by the question. In other types of paper a student should be clear that such questions are not short essays. The report technique – part essay, part draft – is the best technique to use.

Major strategic points of primary importance (and numbered appropriately) are very important. A sentence or two of introduction should be followed by 'a list' of secondary and tertiary information, arranged either vertically or horizontally, before the answer is concluded by a further sentence or two.

Key techniques: The 'List' and 'The Layering Model.'

3. DATA RESPONSE QUESTIONS

Data Response questions require you to read, understand and interpret data presented statistically in the form of graphs, tables, indices etc. Although the information is presented visually and graphically the requirements are not different, in any major way, to more traditional styles of question.

What is involved?

Definition and explanation of concepts are the core of such questions. Additionally examiners would expect some of the following:

a) Descriptions and interpretations of statistical relationships or associations illustrated by the data.
b) Explanations of textbook theories (or exceptions to them) illustrated by the data.
c) Discussion of ideas arising out of the data.
d) Evaluation of the data to calculate trends and relativities: It is always best to use % to measure changes.
e) Discriminate between alternative explanations.

Writing your answers

1. READ
   The questions and read all the messages. You must respond to the exact question.
2. THINK AND PLAN IN ROUGH
   Make assumptions, select information, weigh its importance and judge its impact on the reader.
3. BE 'CONCEPT' ORIENTATED
   Do not just paraphrase. Apply concepts from the syllabus to the data. Test them, explain them and comment on them.
4. CONCLUSION
   There is unlikely to be a single correct answer. Your answer should arise from your logical pattern of thought.

Note also that the questions are not equal challenges, There will be some (worth one or two marks) which are there to help you start – don't overlook these.

4. CASE STUDIES

A Case Study is a story about specific situations. Once read, students will be asked to answer questions arising from the case. The format of case studies may appear to be different to other papers, but the knowledge and many of the skills required to perform well are the same. The overall approach to a case study should be disciplined and logical.

1. Reading (allow at least 20 minutes)
Skim-read the case first to obtain an overview of the story. Read the questions next, making sure that all the messages, both directional and technical, are both seen and understood. Then-re-read the text, organising and patterning the information as you go by underlining and annotating.

2. Time Management
At the beginning should remain quite flexible. An initial budget might be set by reference to the number of marks awarded to each question. However, if there are any questions you decide not to attempt, time will need to be re-allocated according to the student's tactical plan.

3. Order
A good idea is to begin with the question you can do best/quickest to acquire confidence as well as a positive time bank. Another tactic is to begin with the question which has the most marks allocated to it, taking care not to allow time to run over budget.

4. Answers
It is very easy to be carried away by the storyline and forget to use the knowledge from the syllabus. A way around this is to behave in a fashion similar to a doctor examining a patient; to read the details of the case as symptoms and relate them to concepts:

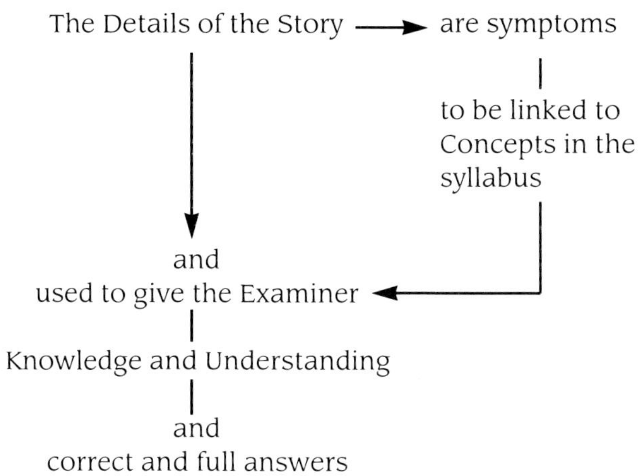

The most important techniques are:
Ask the right questions
Be concept orientated
The Inverted Pyramid
The Layering Model

All answers should display logical reasoning, balanced evaluation and clear arguments which support and justify the conclusions chosen.

Unless a question is totally quantitative, answers should contain:

- An overview introduction (Use the Inverted Pyramid)
- Definition of concept(s)
- Analysis – what is the question about/going on here?
- Linking ideas into a pattern
- Follow through – state both cause and effect.

5. ANALYSIS QUESTIONS

Analysis questions, often found in science and quantitative papers use similar techniques to those of data response papers.

Analysis of the question and its information is the first step, using the technique of 'Asking the right questions.' Next, develop relevant criteria by which to make a judgement, test the range of alternatives before arriving at a final conclusion.

6. MULTIPLE CHOICE QUESTIONS

Multiple Choice questions test objectively a student's knowledge of the 'nuts and bolts' of a syllabus – the theories, concepts, principles, formulae and techniques. Although there are different types of Multiple Choice questions.

Single Completion
  Tests definitions/direct questions
  Only one correct answer is possible
Assertion-Reason
  Tests comprehension and reasoning
  Both assertion and reason have to be true

The most common is the Multiple Completion in which a statement (known as the stem) is followed by four or five options, only one of which is correct, the others being distractors. Always, read the whole question, including all the choices.

Techniques
Multiple Choice questions are an ideal place to use the technique of: 'Ask the right questions, you get the right answer!'

Use rough paper to doodle – ideas, relationships, calculations, and graphical illustrations of stated principles, to see if they look right.

Examine first the stem:
- What theory/concept is being asked about?
- Can I visualise what is meant/doodle on rough paper.
- Compare your understanding with the stem; do you agree or disagree?
- Without looking at the options, try to arrive at an answer.

Examine next, the alternatives:
Your strategy should be to narrow the range of options by progressively reducing the range of choice. Do this by asking:

- Are there any options which can be discounted immediately because they are nonsense.
- Of the options remaining are there any which are largely or totally incorrect? Discount those that are.
- If you are left with more than one 'correct' alternative, choose the option which maximises – gives the best, widest, most complete answer.

In a subject such as Economics, the theories of which use equilibrium based models, the following pattern might be employed.

Changes in a model move through four stages

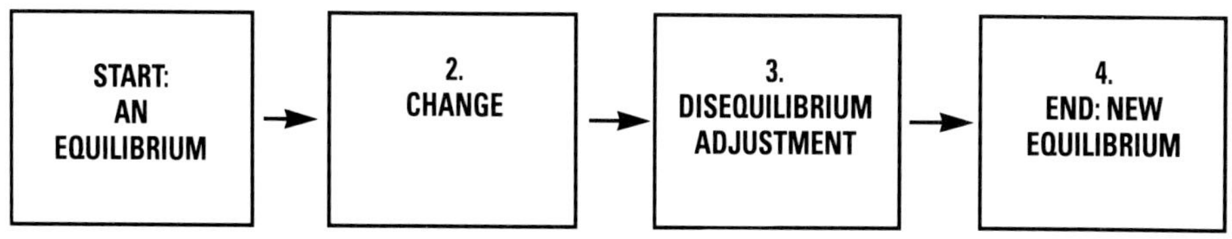

Strategies in the Exam Room:

ORDER AND PACE are vital.

Skim through the whole paper very quickly. Mark the questions you know you can do easily and quickly.
Do these questions first.
Do next, the questions you know you can do, but which will take a little time.
Do third, the questions which will be a struggle.
Do last, those questions about which you know little or nothing!
(It is a fact that a person who knows absolutely nothing can achieve around 10-12%).

If any one question is taking too long – is becoming a 'time robber' – move to another question and return later.

7. WRITING 'A REPORT FORM' ANSWER

Writing a 'report form' answer is quite different to writing an essay, or a short answer. It MUST be written in a very specific way. Presentation is very much a part of the answer.

PRESENTATION

1. Headings
2. Writing each section:
   i Each section should be properly numbered.
   ii The writing of each section should proceed in a series of numbered sections.
3. The 'Report' should be signed and dated.
4. Any statistical information should be appended at the end of the report in a series of Appendices, all of which should be properly numbered and labelled.

SEQUENCE

START:
A HEADING

REPORT ON ______________________________

WRITTEN BY ______________________________

POSITION ______________________________

INTRODUCTION:
The purpose is to explain the terms of reference. ie: WHY the report has been prepared and written.

METHODS:
The methods of data collection and analysis should be clearly stated.

THE FINDINGS:
This is the major part of the report.

CONCLUSION:
A clear set of conclusions should be given.

RECOMMENDATIONS:
A set of recommendations should be given based on the findings and the conclusions.

ESSAY WRITING

Essays are personal statements written to impress the reader with your knowledge and understanding your thoughtfulness, and your ability to communicate effectively. They offer the student an opportunity to show a wide range of abilities:

Writing essays in an exam, when all the performance elements are present is very different to writing during course work. While different skills and techniques are required, the overall process is the same:

THINKING --------------------PLANNING -------------------- WRITING

An essay is an exercise in self discovery, a chance to work out ideas and arguments on paper, to develop not only the way you think, but the way you express your thoughts.

1. WRITING ESSAYS DURING COURSE WORK

INITIAL ANALYSIS

AIM
What is the objective of the title:

ANALYSIS
What are the key phrases/concepts?

THINKING

INFORMATION

What information is necessary?
What part of my notes/texts/books are needed?
Where do I look for additional information

INNOVATE/IDEAS

Question your information
Group, pattern, organise information

PLANNING

Pre-Plan:	Use rough paper
Decide:	The purpose of the information The hierarchy of the information Main ideas/concepts – supporting Detail and examples
Decide:	Signposts to tell your reader where you are at and where you are going

ORGANISATION AND STRUCTURE

Introduction:	Use to Show your Knowledge Define concepts briefly Explain relevancy of concepts to essay
Mainstream:	Use to Show Use of Knowledge Develop main themes/analysis Signposts – linking sentences/paragraphs
Conclusion:	Two or three sentences to tie the loose ends together.
Checklist:	Length, balance, does conclusion answer the question.

End Planning by writing formal draft.

WRITING
Write from your draft not your books/notes
Spell correctly: Bad spelling distracts the reader and creates an impression of lack of care and impatience.
Style: Keep simple, clear, precise.
Punctuation: Helps style
Relevance: How well have you answered the question?

REVIEW AND ASSESS

2. WRITING ESSAYS IN EXAMS

THE IMPORTANCE

This varies from subject to subject, being greater in arts subjects than in the sciences. Eric Evans, Professor of History at Lancaster University writes: 'as many as three quarters of available marks are awarded to timed essays. The conclusion is inescapable. Anyone who does not devote a considerable part of preparation time to writing essays against the clock is throwing away marks.'

The replacement of 'O' Levels by GCSE means that many 'A' Level students have to learn how to write essays during their course. Therefore, during the Familiarisation Stage timed essays should be practised at least once a week.

THE IMPRESSION

Essays are opportunities to create a good impression. Three key words are vital: 'Relevance, Selectivity and Precision'

'Examiners are much more like to be seduced by crisp, precise and relevant writing, than worn down by attrition, or blasted into awarding a high grade by a fusillade of facts.' *(Eric Evans)*

THE TECHNIQUES

Although the writing process is the same as for an essay during course work crucially, the balance is different. Much 'thinking' should already have been done during the Familiarisation and Learning Stages with the result that this part of the process can be truncated.

Pressure from 'time' is a major problem during exams. Students are expected to 'think, plan – and write.' It helps to remember that time has been allowed for all these activities. No matter the pressure, never be tempted to omit 'Planning', 10-15% of time should always be devoted to this phase. Keep plans simple, precise and relevant. It is detailed plans which waste time.

When you begin to write – write fast – using the following sequence:

1. READ THE QUESTION
- Underline key phrases

2. ANALYSIS
- What type of question is it? (See below pp ??? for additional detail).
- What knowledge is needed?
- What concept(s) are dealt with?
- What part of your notes are required?
- Remember to use the 'Inverted Pyramid model'. Start wide and become narrower!

3. PLANNING
- Make sure the plan is organised and there is a pattern, but don't waste time writing much detail or unecessary words such as Introduction, Mainstream and Conclusion.

Three typical patterns:-

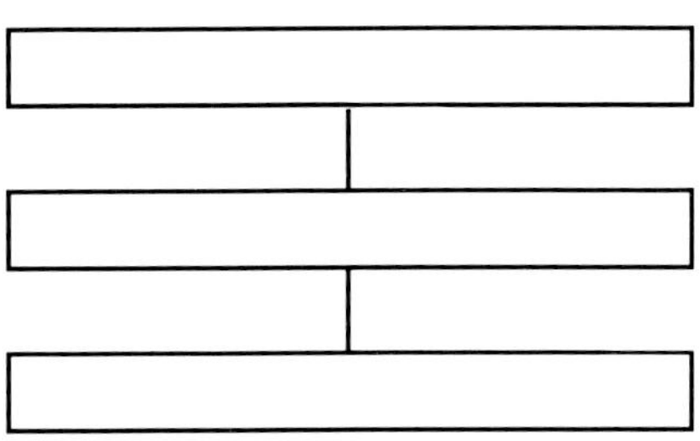

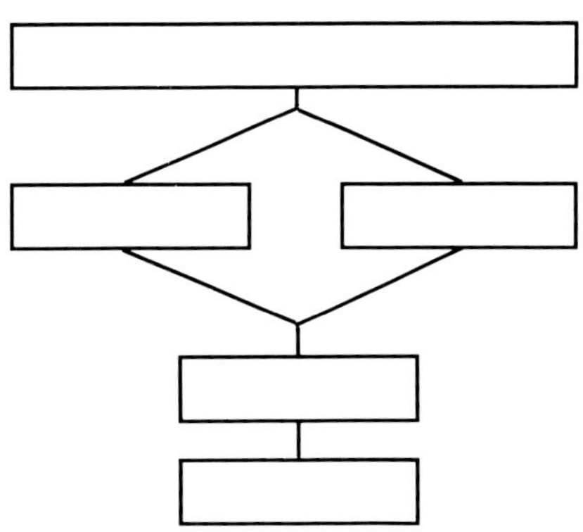

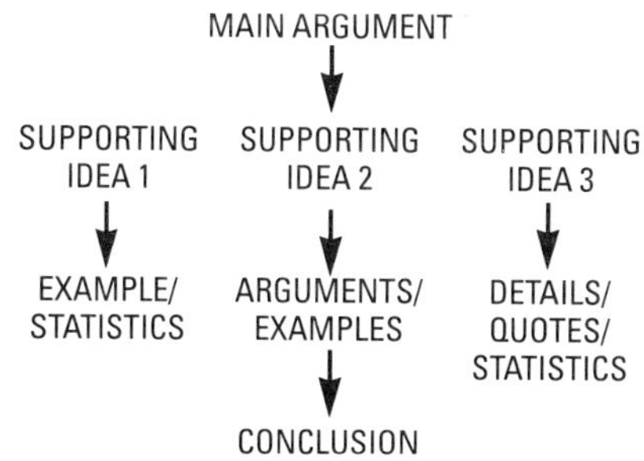

4. WRITE THE ESSAY
   The examiner expects:

   Knowledge and Use of Knowledge

   Relevance and Selection

   Organisation and fluent expression

   So –

   a) Lay the foundation:
      - Re-state the question as a statement
      - Define the concepts of the question
      - Explain their relevance

   b) Expand and Apply:
      - Apply concepts to answer specific question
        remember: define any new terms used
      - Reinforce ideas with support
        – details
        – graphs
        – diagrams
      - Support details with examples

   c) Conclusion:
      - Summarise by re-stating the main idea and point of view
      - State how you proved, supported, defended, arrived at your conclusion

ESSAY DIRECTION WORDS

IF YOU ARE ASKED TO:	YOU SHOULD DO THE FOLLOWING
Account for	Answers question why? Evaluate, take a point of view
Analyse	Break down or separate a problem or situation into separate factors and/or relationships. Draw a conclusion, make a judgement, or make clear the relationship you see based on your breakdown.
Categorise	Place items under headings already labelled by your teacher.
Classify	Organise a pattern of items in related groups.
Compare	State how things are alike or not alike.
Consider	Invite you to hold a view.
Contrast	Tell how things are different.
Criticise	Make a judgement of the work of art or literature and support your judgement.
Deduce	Trace the course; derive a conclusion by reasoning.
Defend	Give enough details to prove the statement.
Define	Give the meaning.
Describe	Give an account in words: trace the outline or present a picture.
Diagram	Use pictures, graphs, charts, mind maps & flow charts to show relationships of details to main ideas.
Discuss	Consider the various points present all sides of the issue and then arrive at a conclusion.
Distinguish	Tell how this is different from others similar to it.
Enumerate	List all possible items.
Evaluate	Make a judgement based on the evidence and support it; give the good and bad points.
Explain	The question why. Give reasons or causes.
How	As for explain.
Illustrate	Make clear by examples, pictures, charts, diagrams or concrete examples.
Interpret	Express your thinking by giving the meaning as you see it.
Justify	Give some evidence/reasons supporting your statement with facts.
List	Write in a numbered fashion.
Outline	Concisely and directly give the main ideas.
Paraphrase	Put in your own words
Predict	Present solutions that could happen if certain variables were present.
Prove	Provide factual evidence to back up the truth of the statment.
Relate	Show the relationship among concepts.
Review	Examine the information critically. Analyse and comment on the important statements.
State	Establish by specifying. Write what you believe and support with evidence.
Summarise	Condense the main points in the fewest words possible.
Synthesise	Combine parts or pieces of an idea, situation or event.
To what extent	Quantify either objectivity or subjectivity
Trace	Describe in steps the progression of something.
Verify	Confirm or establish the truth of accuracy of point of view with supporting examples, evidence and facts.
Why	The reasons for . . .

2. MENTAL SKILLS

TIME MANAGEMENT SCHEDULE

DAILY SCHEDULE

DAY:	TIME	ACTIVITY PLANNED	ACTIVITY REPORT
PERIOD 1	0700		
	0800		
PERIOD 2	0900		
	1000		
	1100		
	1200		
LUNCH	1300		
	1400		
	1430		
PERIOD 3	1500		
	1600		
	1630		
TEA			
PERIOD 4	1700		
	1800		
	1900		
SUPPER			
PERIOD 5	2000		
	2100		
	2200		
	2300		

HOW TO MAKE USE OF YOUR ANSWERS TO QUESTIONNAIRE ONE

Each of the questions on Questionnaire 1 refers to either a mental skill or a technical skill involved in learning and studying. All questions deal with Learning Methods except those listed below:

Questions 1 and 2: Self Confidence

3 and 4: Goal Setting

5 and 9: Time Management

7 and 8: Concentration

Those questions which have been answered 4 or 5 can be considered 'a relative strength.' Those answered 1, 2 or 3 need more work, the urgency being illustrated by your own relative concern.

PLANNING THE ROUTE MAP OF YOUR PREPARATION

Start with:
Analysis of – Yourself / The Tasks

THE ROUTE MAP:

THE OVERALL PLAN OF CONTROL

YOUR PLAN FOR YOURSELF

1. Learn to be a Winner
2. Self Talk
3. Motivation
4. Goal Setting
5. Concentration
6. Relaxation
7. Stress Control
8. Physical Plan

YOUR PLAN FOR YOUR STUDY PROGRAMME

1. Control Time
   How long?
   When during each day?
   How long each session?
   How to control?
2. Control Distractions
3. Design a Personal Study Place
4. Preparation over all of the subject

YOUR PLAN FOR TECHNICAL/ ACADEMIC EXCELLENCE

1. Organise the Syllabus
2. Prioritise the Syllabus
3. Write the Performance Script

PLAN FOR EXAM PERFORMANCE

1. Familiarise
2. Simulation
3. Coping Strategy
4. 'What If . . .?'

THE REST OF YOUR LIFE

1. What is going on in my life?
2. How important is each activity?
3. How much time do they take up?
4. Which help/which hinder preparation
5. Prioritise
6. Organise
7. Control – jettison!

PLANNING YOUR EXAM PERFORMANCE

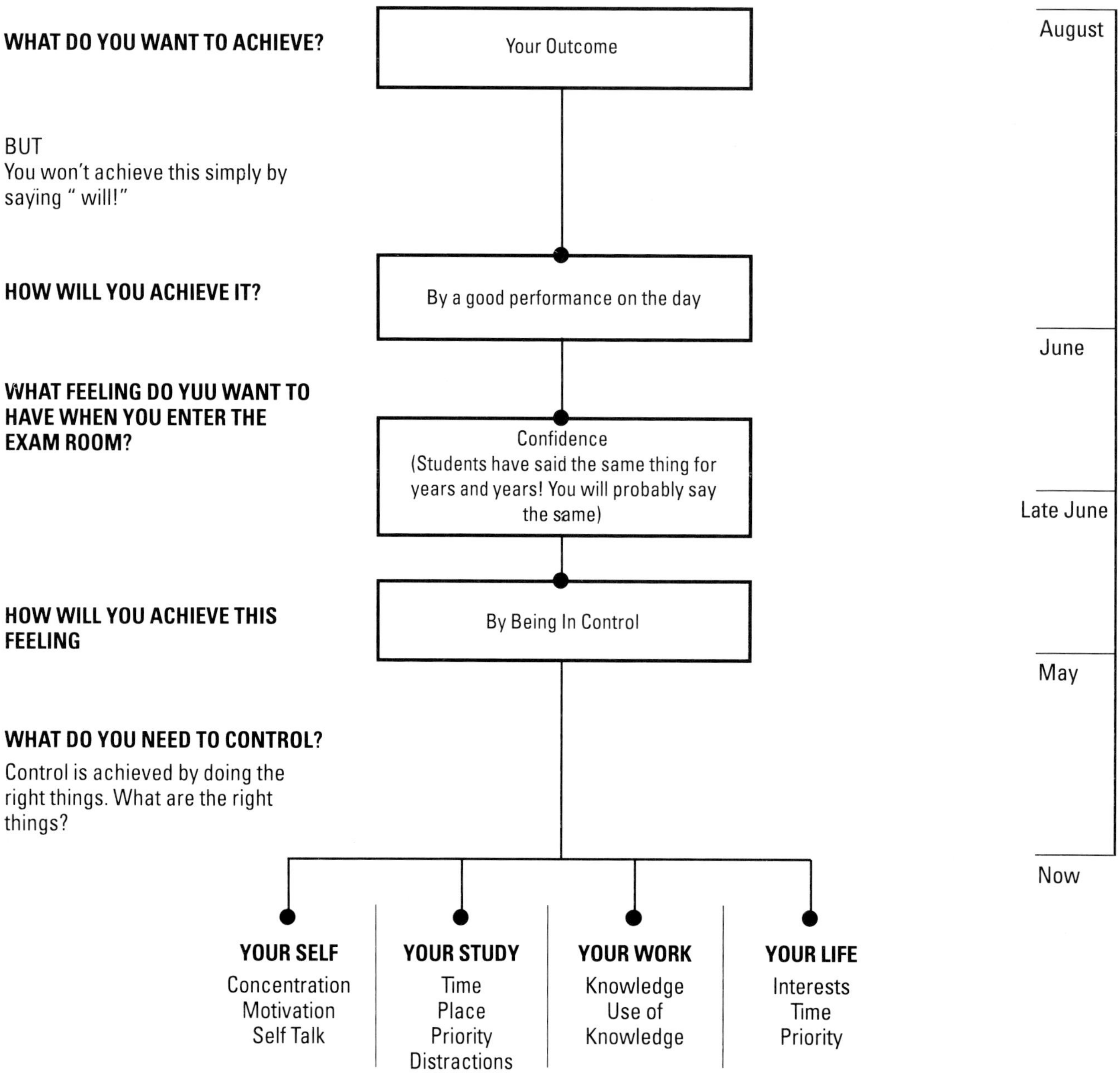

PROBLEM SOLVING MODELS

Many people think they have problems. However, after the use of a coping model, those problems could appear to be much smaller. DON'T PANIC: use one of the two problem solving models given below. Either model works, depending on the individual.

MODEL ONE

1. DEFINE the problem clearly in behavioural terms.
2. BRAINSTORM – generate a wide range of possible alternative courses of action.
3. IMAGINE AND CONSIDER how others might respond if asked to solve a similar problem.
4. EVALUATE pros and cons of each proposed solution.
5. TRY OUT the most acceptable and feasible solution.
6. RECONSIDER the original problem in the light of this attempt at problem solving. (Does the problem look different. Can you see anything positive about the situation?)

MODEL TWO

In working towards getting what you want, you may ask of yourself the following questions.

Go through the process of asking yourself the questions in relationship to what you want.

Notice the effect of asking these questions in this way has on you. It may mean that you don't actually have a problem at all – just you thought you had.

PROBLEM FRAME
What is your problem? (Be very specific)

Why is it a problem?

Why do you have it?

What caused it?

What are your limitations in solving it?

Whose fault is it?

Who is to blame?

Why haven't you solved it yet?

Now repeat the process of questioning for the following. Also notice the effect this has on you.

OUTCOME FRAME
What do you want?

How do you want it to be?

What do you need to get it?

What resources do you already have that will help you get this outcome?

Where are you now?

What is the next step you can take in getting your outcome?

Always be objective about problems. If you are feeling angry, upset, frustrated or emotional in any way, you will NOT be able to solve problems and make clear decisions.

COPING – A SELF HELP APPROACH

If at any time an individual appears to be panicking, or seems snowed under and not coping, the following simple self-help model may help to relieve the tension. Each step can be done either by talking to someone else, or by writing the answers down for yourself.

A SELF-HELP APPROACH TO COPING

Step 1: Know yourself.

Step 2: Relax.

Step 3: Decide what is important.

Step 4: Rally your support system.

Step 5: Keep communicating.

Step 6: Adopt a problem solving approach.

Step 7: Express your feelings through discussion etc.

GLOSSARY OF MENTAL SKILLS

Affirmation A statement, usually to oneself, to state the positive abilities, skills and behaviour.

Anxiety An emotional condition which leads to a troubled state of mind. Anxiety can reveal itself in both physical and mental ways.

Attitude An expression of what we are thinking. The expressed attitude usually has a consistent relationship to behaviour.

Auditory The sense of hearing.

Communication The giving, receiving, imparting or the interchange of information. Using speech, writing, signs, or non-verbal signs.

Concentration The ability to focus on the relevant parts of a task, and shutting out what is irrelevant to the task.

Distractions Stimuli, either internal or external, which disturb or affect the concentration.

External focus Points of focus outside the body i.e. in the environment or in other people.

Goal A goal is something which the performer, examinee, business-man, wants to happen. It is the goal which gives the direction for the behaviour to achieve that particular goal.

Goal-setting A technique which involves setting certain goals as a progression to achieving, improvement and success in performance. This technique is considered to be one of the most effective methods of remaining motivated!

Internal focus Points of focus to do with the body or mind, which disturb or affect the concentration. Kinaesthetic sense.

Kineasthetic sense The signals and internal information which the body is constantly giving about balance, movement and what the feelings are like when moving.

Mental rehearsal A process where the performer watches themselves on a screen in 'the mind's eye.' There is usually a specific end in view, and it should always be positive. It may involve the use of all the senses. (Touch, taste, kin-easthetic, sight, and hearing).

Motivation The intensity and direction of behaviour. i.e. the individual either approaches or avoids a situation and decides on the amount of effort to accomplish the behaviour).

Negative Implying denial through thinking, speaking or writing. Expressing or lacking positive beliefs.

Physiological Relating to the functioning of the human body.

Positive Confident in opinion. Have a self belief in one's own ability.

Reinforcement Negative or positive information following behaviour or an action. (Such information can be given by the individual or other people).

Relaxation The ability to allow the muscles to do nothing and 'letting go'.

Schedule Timetable, or programme of planned events.

Self concept An image of what we think we are, what others think of us, what we would like to be, and what we think we can achieve.

Self confidence The belief and self assurance in one's own abilities.

Self talk A method involving speaking to ourselves or 'listening' to one's own internal thought processes. 'If accurate and in touch with reality, we function well. If they are irrational and untrue, then anxiety and emotional disturbance occur.

Strategy A plan of action.

Time management The careful planning of how the individual uses time

Visual Concerned with seeing, using the sight.

3. PRACTICES

MOCK EXAMINATIONS

'MOCKS' ARE FOR YOUR BENEFIT – NO ONE ELSE'S. Approach them: 'Lightheartedly but seriously.' Lightheartedly because whatever the outcome, nothing really disastrous can befall you; seriously because if you are to take full advantage of the opportunity offered by 'mocks', there has to be a serious intent. 'Mocks' are an opportunity to practice every fragment of performance:

- Practice controlling yourself during preparation.
- Practice controlling yourself during performance and afterwards
- Assessing how successful your control has been!

No other occasion offers the opportunity to experience a week or ten days of exams, when all your subjects are examined together. This is the only time you will be able to simulate, as closely as possible, the real experience of performing on the exam stage. More important than just a practice, 'mocks' are a dress rehearsal, the only one you will have!

Although control over the knowledge and technical skills of your subject may be uppermost in your minds, much more important at this stage is – YOU HANDLING YOURSELF!

THE TIMING OF MOCKS WILL DETERMINE YOUR APPROACH

Mocks take place at a variety of times between December and May, between 5/6 months before final performance and one month. Exactly when your mocks take place will have an important bearing on both your goal setting and your strategy and tactics.

The further away from final performance your mocks are, the more of an initial practice they become and the more lightheartedly they can be treated. The nearer final performance they are, the more seriously they have to be treated.

PREPARATION NEEDS REHEARSING AS WELL AS PERFORMANCE

Whenever the date of your 'mocks', time management will always be a key element. Right from the beginning, determine that you will practice controlling time.

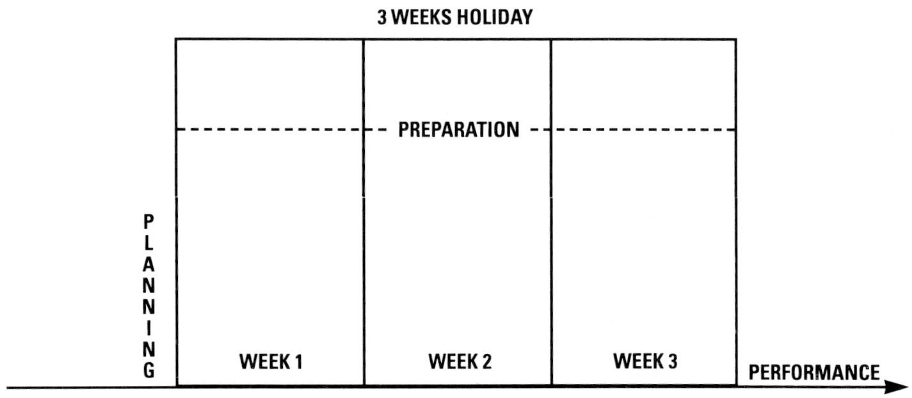

Draw a preparation and performance calendar which gives a view of the whole period. Divide this into three stages – Planning, Preparation and Performance.

REVISION TIMETABLE

MONDAY	13th Back to School	20th Final Accounts	27th Costing	2nd Stock Control
TUESDAY		Maths Trial	Design Breakdown	C.P.A.
WEDNESDAY		Maths Trial Normal Distribution	CIA	Blending
THURSDAY			Index Numbers	Depreciation
FRIDAY	END OF TERM		NEW YEARS EVE	Simulation
SATURDAY		CHRISTMAS DAY	NEW YEAR	Blending
SUNDAY	Maths	BOXING DAY	Forecasting	

This timetable is just one example. Other students might draw it quite differently – each of us has our own way of visualising time. Plan to revise systematically through the weeks ahead. A great many alternative plans, determined by commitments, interests and motivation, are not only possible but acceptable. Your programme has to be your decision.

HAVE A PLANNING PERIOD IN ADVANCE OF PREPARATION

Use this to decide:

- Your Philosophy
- Your Strategy
- Your Goals
- Your Start Point

YOUR PHILOSOPHY

One philosophy favoured by some students is 'to do no revision at all and see how they get on.' While this is a perfectly acceptable philosophy if mocks are a long time away from final preparation, it is extremely risky if mocks are but a few weeks away. It also has the disadvantage of allowing no preparation practice.

Another, perhaps because of lack of preparation time, is to revise widely but superficially. This allows some preparation practice but in much too loose a fashion to be really useful. A third is to try to take control of a limited range of the syllabus – perhaps the parts you like the best, the parts you are good at, or the most important sections of the syllabus.

YOUR GOALS

Goals must be personal to the student. Whatever they are, decide them at the beginning, write them down so that you can keep them in front of you throughout the practice period, and review them honestly and purposefully at the end. Set an outcome goal first – what you want to achieve at the end.

Bear in mind that at this stage you will not be as well prepared as you will be in your final performance – you won't have as much time to prepare and whatever anyone tells you, these exams are not as serious as the real ones.

Consider carefully the time you intend devoting to preparation, how familiar you are with the syllabus already, and select goals which are appropriate to your ability, your preparedness and your attitude towards this practise performance. The more familiar you are and/or the more time you will devote to preparation, the higher should be your expected outcome.

Don't set goals like 'I will do as well as I can' or 'I'll see how I get on and then set them later.' Make your goals:

Specific and Positive
Realistic
Measurable
Personal
Under Your Control
Short Term

For instance:

I want a B grade in: the topics you have identified as the most likely to be examined.

I want an A grade in: the areas about which I feel most confidence.

I want an E grade in: the areas I feel least confidence.

Today I will finish off the wives of Henry the Eighth.

I will go skiing for a week but when I return I will start revising straightaway and will keep it up for the following ten days.

YOUR STRATEGY
Decide your strategy and your strategic goals that will determine the broad sweep of your programme – whether you will work intermittently through the period, a little each day, or for one complete period at the end; whether you will work for short work periods or long; how you will apportion your time between each of your subjects and each area of their syllabus.

YOUR START POINT
Decide in advance a formal start point. Start then and maintain your programme afterwards.

TACTICS DURING PREPARATION
Tactics – the daily practices and behaviours that determine the successful achievement of your strategy and thus your outcome – require performance or activity goals to be set continually, each week, each day perhaps even each hour.

Be Active
- Don't be a passive reviser. Always be doing something – writing, memorising, practising questions, sometimes against the clock.

Stay in the Present
- Learn to focus on what is happening and what needs to be controlled 'now'.

Organise the Syllabus
- Try to organise the total syllabus to gain an idea of how big it is and how it fits together.

Control Subject Areas
- Assess their importance and choose a few to prepare in depth.

TACTICS DURING PERFORMANCE
No one should ever go into a performance thinking 'it will be alright on the night.' Always have a plan which includes both the pre-performance period (the hours immediately before the exam itself) as well as the exam itself.

Plan to control yourself
- Your feelings, emotions and reactions.

Plan to control your work
- Your knowledge, skills and organisation

ASSESSING THE SUCCESS OF YOUR MOCKS
The result you achieve will be one element of assessment – but only one. Much more important will be your personal judgement of how successful you were controlling both your preparation and performance, relative to the goals you set and the strategy you employed.

Recognise what did and what did not work for you during preparation and performance, and assess your success:

Learning to Cope
- Remember situations when control over yourself had to be deliberately exerted and how successful you were.

Learning the importance of Pre Performance Routines

- Those routines adopted prior to performance which have an effect on how well you perform.

Learning to Assess Feelings

- 'How you feel' in different parts of the performance situation, particularly immediately before and during performance, and when things do not go precisely according to plan!

Learning the importance of Performance

- In determining the final outcome.
  Use this knowledge to plan your final preparation and performance.

PRACTICE EXAMS ARE NOT TESTS: THEY ARE PRACTICES!

THE PHILOSOPHY
A Practice Exam is not 'a test' in the way a mock exam is. It is a practice performance. The result, although important as a performance indicator, is less important than your evaluation of the total performance.

ORGANISATION
Practice exams are best organised by an institution because the environment in which the actual exam will be taken can be simulated exactly. Simulating without the help of an institution is more difficult but, to a greater or lesser degree, still possible.

Decide a time within a specific day for the practice. Set aside a suitable room for the purpose, and simulate as many elements of the exam environment that you can, the most important being temperature, noise levels, working area and the presence of an invigilator.

HOW TO USE TO YOUR ADVANTAGE
Precede the practice with a day of exam preparation and a pre-performance period.

Decide a pre-performance routine and an exam strategy. Set realistic goals which are appropriate to your level of knowledge. Evaluate all three afterwards.

During the practice, focus on yourself, yourself as a performer. Practice controlling the elements of performance in particular planning, pace and time, and pay particular attention to your feelings, and emergencies.

After the practice, sit down with a sheet of paper to evaluate each stage of the performance. Provided that you analyse and evaluate realistically, your future performance will be enhanced.

4. PARENTS

SOME TIPS FOR PARENTS – HOW TO HELP AT HOME?

When 'A' level students were recently asked what were their chief distractions during revision and exam time, one of the chief answers proved to be PARENTS.

THE ROLE OF THE PARENTS AT EXAM TIME.
The first thing that you have to realise is that on the whole your parents only want the best for you, and of course they want you to succeed and do well in your exams. Not only is it seen to be satisfying for them that their son or daughter has succeeded, but it is also another stage of development successfully reached.

Your parent's role is particularly important at this important time for you because your involvement and enjoyment during the exam period is not simply the responsibility of the school and the teachers, but it becomes a shared responsibility between you, your parents, and the school. The support shown by your parents at this time is crucial to your overall well-being and confidence in the exam performance. Not all parents understand what is involved in revising for important exams and therefore the key to a full understanding on both parts, you and your parents, is to share with them your programme, explain what it means to you and then listen to any concerns they may have on your behalf. This approach can help in the following ways.

- It enables your parents to fully understand what you are aiming to do and the goals you want to achieve.
- It helps your parents to become informed about the exact nature of your performance programme, and the implications for them. (It may mean that you would like to have your meal served in your room, or, you may not wish to eat with the family because it doesn't fit in with your schedule. If you share a room with a brother or sister it may mean that you have to spend a lot of time in the library and this may have implications for parents, brothers and sisters and perhaps the normal daily routine of the home).
- It enables your parents to understand what is expected of you and as a consequence what is expected of them.
- It helps you to understand the concerns of your parents.
- It helps to establish good, supportive lines of communication between you, your parents, and the school.
- It means that you can obtain support from your parents in helping to make your performance programme work.

SHARE IT, DISCUSS IT, HELP THEM TO UNDERSTAND

COMMUNICATION IS THE KEY. TRY TO UNDERSTAND EACH OTHER

Parents always want to help, and there are many anecdotal stories about how parents apply pressure to their children out of ignorance because they don't think you're working hard enough, or because you are off to play tennis again, that's three times this week! Why are you listening to pop music, wouldn't it be better to spend your time doing some more revision? The exams are only 2 weeks away, can you really afford to take part of this week-end off? There are many more to which I'm sure you can add. Write them below, don't get upset about it, all you have to do is to inform your parents and talk to them about your goals, your expectations, your schedule of work, your free time which is so precious to you. If you keep your side of the bargain then they will almost certainly keep theirs, because they want to support you.

It is very evident that parents are important people and they offer you a great deal of support in many ways, but sometimes they are uncertain as to the exact nature of that support. As much of the recent research in development psychology tells us, how parents behave is often determined by your actions.

Guidelines for parents:

IN ORDER FOR YOUR OFFSPRING TO HAVE THE OPPORTUNITY OF NOT ONLY SUCCESS BUT ALSO ENJOYMENT DURING THIS TIME YOU SHOULD:

- Your son or daughter is going to be engaged in some very hard work which at times will cause anxiety, tension and short tempers! At other times there may be swings in behaviour ranging from downright rudeness, surliness, through to a kind of euphoria. They may make demands on the family which appear to be quite out of proportion.
- Try to see the exam involvement not just as passing or failing but as a challenge in which the nature of the performance becomes very important. Try to recognise that their endeavours are maximised by your understanding, guidance and support rather than coercion.
- Try to understand, through communication what is going to be involved in the 'revision' period and what your role should be.
- Try to become a good listener, so that you can begin to establish the student's feelings when he/she is talking to you. In this way you will then be able to give 'feedback' about these feelings and empathise with the student.
- Establish trust between you. Show that you trust each other and that each of you in turn can express your feelings freely without blame or hurt. Communicate that you are also interested in the real person and not just in the outcome of any examinations.
- Try to be positive. This means managing the very difficult behaviour patterns without reducing the child's self-esteem. If you have negative thoughts and feelings try to change them into positive ones before you speak. Are you as a parent more negative than positive at this time? If so try to have a variety of positive phrases and words ready to use when needed.
- Try to be clear about your expectancies of your son or daughter. It is important to communicate such expectancies without being seen to preach or giving commands. Encourage the young person to feel independent and that you have confidence in their ability to succeed at their level.

REMEMBER – AVOID SETTING TOO HIGH EXPECTANCIES OF YOUR CHILD'S ABILITY. ALWAYS BE SUPPORTIVE OF THEM AT THEIR LEVEL AND ENCOURAGE THEM TO WORK HARD AT THEIR PERFORMANCE.

5. ADDRESSES OF EXAMINATION BOARDS

GCE EXAMINING BOARDS

ASSOCIATED EXAMINING BOARD
Stag Hill House
Guildford
Surrey
GU2 5XJ
Tel: 0482 506506

UNIVERSITY OF LONDON EXAMINATIONS AND ASSESSMENT COUNCIL (ULEAC)
Stewart House
32 Russell Square
London
WC1B 5DN
Tel: 071 331 4000

JOINT MATRICULATION BOARD
Manchester
M15 6EU
Tel: 061 953 1180

UNIVERSITY OF CAMBRIDGE LOCAL EXAMINATIONS SYNDICATE
Syndicate Buildings
1 Hills Road
Cambridge
CB1 2EU
Tel: 0223 61111

MIDLAND EXAMINING GROUP
Mill Wharf
Mill Street
Birmingham
B6 4BU
Tel: 021 628 2933

OXFORD AND CAMBRIDGE SCHOOLS EXAMINATION BOARD
(Oxford Office)
Elsfield Way
Oxford
OX2 8EP
Tel: 0865 54421

(Cambridge Office)
Brook House
10 Trumpington Street
Cambridge
CB2 1QB
Tel: 0223 411211

OXFORD DELEGACY OF LOCAL EXAMINATIONS
Ewert Place
Summertown
Oxford
OX2 7BZ
Tel: 0865 54291

WELSH JOINT EDUCATION COMMITTEE
245 Western Avenue
Cardiff
CF5 2YX
Tel: 0222 561231

NORTHERN EXAMINATION AND ASSESSMENT BOARD
Devas Road
Manchester
M15 6EX
Tel: 061 953 1180

SOUTHERN EXAMINING GROUP CENTRAL ADMINISTRATION OFFICE
Stag Hill House
Guildford
Surrey
GU2 5XJ
Tel: 0483 503123

OTHER EXAMINING BODIES

BUSINESS AND TECHNICIAN EDUCATION COUNCIL
Central House
Upper Woburn Place
London
WC1H 0HH
Tel: 071 388 3288

ROYAL SOCIETY OF ARTS EXAMINATION BOARD
Progress House
Westwood Business Park
Westwood Way
Coventry
CV4 8HS
Tel: 0203 470033

NORTHERN IRELAND SCHOOLS EXAMINATION COUNCIL
Beechill House
42 Beechill Road
Belfast
BT8 4RS
Tel: 0232 704666

SCOTTISH EXAMINATION BOARD
Ironmills Road
Dalkeith
Midlothian
EH22 1LE
Tel: 031 663 6601

CITY AND GUILDS OF LONDON INSTITUTE
76 Portland Place
London
W1N 4AA
Tel: 071 580 3050